MW00655474

Get Your ACT* Together

© 2014 by Scholastic Test Prep Publishing, LLC®

Published by Scholastic Test Prep Publishing, LLC
Kenosha, WI

Written by Samantha Young
Contributing Writer: Maureen Swade
Book design by Lisa Fisher
Illustrations by Sam Lidester and Brian Sisson

Printed in the United States of America

ISBN: 978-0-9859447-0-4

Test Prep Seminars® is a registered trademark of
Test Prep Seminars, Inc.
visit: www.testprepseminars.org

*ACT is a registered trademark of ACT, Inc.
ACT was not involved in the production of,
and does not endorse, this book.

table of contents

ACT

CHAPTER 1
Welcome

Okay, first things first…relax; you are going to do just fine! If you're already freaking out, take solace in knowing that you're already ahead of the game just by taking the first step in reading this Test Prep book. Many of your 1.5 million testing-peers this year will be meeting this exam for the very first time on the big day, and *they'll* be experiencing your present panic at the absolute *worst* time possible. Think of this moment of dread…or *terror*…as a release from the inevitable first-timer anxiety.

So, we hear you asking (oh, yeah, we can hear into your head!) "why on earth should I take the SAT or ACT anyway? Isn't that what grade point averages are for—to designate who is a smart student?" Well now, smarty pants, let Test Prep school you on something: high schools are drastically different across America—and even across town. In one school you are watched like a hawk by fanatical overlords who insist on perfection, while at another school they let students wander off campus willy nilly and cheat openly on tests. You're probably not in the lucky latter group ... sorry. On the other hand, if you do attend a lazy, cheater-friendly school you might not be quite the excellent student you think you are. And that 4.3 GPA you have? Yeah, it has nothing on the 3.8 earned at the horrible "lockdown prison torture school" mentioned earlier.

So, universities, colleges, and the government colluded to devise these evil standardized tests to "level the playing field." These test scores, along with your school record, tend to be more accurate than just your GPA alone. Think of it this way and you may warm up to the idea…

We all know one of "those" kids at school…you know, the one who always seems to get just a little extra special treatment due to his highly-honed knack of brown-nosing? This is the kid who somehow manages to befriend every teacher, TA, secretary, nurse, attendance officer, lunchroom attendant, and custodian in the school…and then sits back and benefits from all the resulting advantages of doing so. Doesn't that just *burn* you? Well, here's good news: this little brown-noser will have no advantage on ACT testing day. The ACT proctors know of these brown-nosers, too, and they are cold and emotionless to such antics. (At least they're consistent!) This is good for you. *Finally*…a fair fight in which all the brown-noser's cute, "kissing-up antics" mean nothing!

PROCTOR

NOTES:

So, congratulations on taking your first step to leveling the playing field! We here at Test Prep Seminars are hip to the ACT folks' tricky test devices. Our strategies and practice questions are designed with the sole purpose of simplifying the otherwise intimidating three-hour-long ACT exam—just think of us as your secret "test phobia therapists." We build and reinforce time-management and study skills, offer both general as well as very specific test-taking strategies, establish familiarity with question types and presentations, exercise the problem-solving and analytical skills that are key to mastering the American College Test (ACT), and introduce anxiety-reduction techniques to help YOU achieve your full potential. So sit back, relax, and allow us to navigate you calmly through the world of pre-college testing anxiety.

With three million students applying to college each year, your ACT score is critical. For admission officers and scholarship committees, each ACT point you gain will boost you ahead of approximately 100,000 other students nationwide. That's right: 1 point and you're more desirable to colleges than 100,000 other students (psst, colleges express their desire through acceptance letters and *free money*). Interested? We thought you might be. To help you gain this favor in the competitive market of education, Test Prep Seminars' goal is to help you achieve your highest possible score!

NOTES:

After reading this text, check out our TPS workbook, which serves as an excellent complement to this book. It has tons of practice tests containing detailed answers and explanations for your studying pleasure! Complete some practice tests as if they were the real deal: isolate yourself, sit still, adhere to time limits, and *don't cheat*. We know this sounds like self-inflicted torture, but this training method will help you to normalize the writhing pain that accompanies the ACT (you know, the same way that training to be a Mixed Martial Arts fighter makes you forget just how much you hate being punched in the face). So bring on the pain and get to drilling those practice questions!

NOTES:

When you're done with the practice run, make sure to turn to the back of the workbook and read the answer explanations. Even if the answer to a question seemed intuitive at the time, it's extremely valuable to understand the reasoning and pattern behind it. After all, the answer might not jump out at you on exam day, so relying entirely on your gut feeling could prove to be detrimental.

So put in your mouth guard and let's start deconstructing the ACT and its trickery.

(Wait, should you be wearing your mouth guard or your thinking cap? Um, let's be safe and have you use both.)

Your future self will thank you. Or it'll thank itself? Or thank the self that it once was? Never mind, this is getting confusing. Just read on…

CHAPTER 2

About the ACT

NOTES:

The ACT was established in 1959 and used nationwide the following year. As we stated earlier, its purpose is to remove ambiguity from grade point averages (GPA) and create a level playing field for college applicants. For a moment, think of it from a college's point of view: how can they trust wildly different high schools to have comparable standards? They can't. One school's star pupil is another's struggling nincompoop. Giving A's to "less-than-great students" is called **grade inflation**, and it throws a monkey wrench into the college admissions machinery.

When choosing between two students, for example, how does The University of Prestige know if Kim's school doles out A's for effort while Marissa's school would have given Einstein's science fair project on his mass-energy equivalence formula a nice little *runner-up* ribbon? By establishing **standardized** college admission tests, universities can differentiate grade inflation from dedication and reserve classroom seats for true scholars.

CONTENT

Unlike an IQ test, the ACT only pulls material from a **typical high school curriculum**; this equates to everyone having an opportunity to attain a commendable score—even those who aren't blessed with IQs that soar far beyond 140. In addition, there are hidden psychological traps designed into the ACT, the most nefarious being *Time Panic*. In addition, extremely tight time constraints and random question difficulty require *any successful test-taker* to know his or her way around the exam. The three-hour American College Test consists of 215 questions: 75 in English, 60 in math, 40 in reading, and 40 in science. Additionally, there is an optional writing section in which students must compose an essay on a proposed societal issue. The strictly enforced time allotments for each section break down like this:

Time

> **English:** 45 minutes (36 seconds per question)
> **Math:** 60 minutes (60 seconds per question)
> **Reading:** 35 minutes (52.5 seconds per question)
> **Science:** 35 minutes (52.5 seconds per question)
> **Writing:** 30 minutes to compose one essay

Do the ACT people really think they can fully test competency on these subjects in these tiny time frames? Are they *insane*? Ok, so maybe not INSANE…just perhaps a bit devious. They know that giving you too little time will expose flaws in your memory and problem solving skills, your exhaustion or sleep deprivation will reveal itself, or you will panic. Cruel, isn't it?

ACT's dirty little secret:

THERE'S NO TIME

Fortunately, while these time limitations may seem daunting, the exam itself is actually quite predictable and hence, easily navigable—*if* you know your way. So while you may feel that spending the "best years of your life" on extra studying is a waste, consider this: do you want all of that hard work you put into your high school career to come off as four years of acing Home Ec? We didn't think so. Plus, if you get into The University of Prestige and make it to your dream job, you have yet to taste your golden years. (We like to think that they taste like cupcakes—extra sprinkles.)

SCORING

Scoring is based on a nationwide curve. Each section of the exam receives a subject area score (calculated by counting the number of correctly answered questions) which is scaled against a national average; the highest raw scores then set the standard for the perfect ACT score of 36. Lastly, the average of all four sections represents your composite score, the score that potential universities first view. Of the 1.5 million students to take the test in 2009, ACT.org reported that fewer than 0.1%—that's under fifteen hundred of them, by the way—scored a 36, while the average score was a more modest 21.1.

NOTES:

The conversion method for raw-to-composite score is undisclosed, so understanding the true meaning of your ACT score can be a bit difficult. The ACT committee did, however, release the following information regarding percentile rankings and scores for 2014:

Score	English	Math	Reading	Science	Composite
35	99	99	99	99	99
30	92	95	90	96	95
25	78	79	75	83	79
20	50	51	48	47	49
15	25	14	20	16	17
10	6	1	2	2	1

A score of 30, for example, has an average English percentile ranking of 92. This means the test-taker performed equal to or better than 92% of other students who had taken the ACT and was outdone by only 8%.

So, even though we can't tell you *exactly* how your ACT score works, we *do* know how to make it work for you.

PRESENTING (OR RESENTING) YOUR SCORE

Pay close attention here! The ACT registration form contains boxes for school codes, but they are *not* used to identify you and are *not* mandatory. The ACT utilizes private information such as your social security number to verify that you are actually you. (*And not that really, really smart kid you bribed with homemade chocolate chip cookies!*) Those school code boxes, on the other hand, are your way of telling the ACT organization to share your scores with your high school and/or universities.

We advise students to refrain from providing any school codes whatsoever during the registration process. Leaving the school code section blank allows students to view their scores prior to sending them off—or more importantly, *not* sending them off—to the College of High Standards. While this option will cost an extra $9 to $13, it spares you the woe of having sent the embarrassing 10 you'd received due to the unfortunate and unforeseeable consequences of bringing Squeeks, your pet hamster, along for good luck. After learning your lesson (no, Squeeks won't stay preoccupied with a carrot for three hours), you'll be able to send *only*

the spectacular 33 you earned during a productive stint of inner peace (much easier to achieve without an adorable rodent chewing through your khakis—but you know that now). Follow our advice here: it puts you in control because this way you can view your scores before deciding to send/not send.

And another lesson for you: while it isn't common practice, some universities allow students to use the subscores from multiple exams. If a student scored a 22 in math and a 25 in English the first time around, and then a 24 in math and a 24 in English the second time around, the admissions department would use the first test's English score (25) and the second test's math score (24) in the application process. Again, this is not a typical process, so please call the admissions office of your prospective university and inquire prior to sending your scores.

RE-TESTING

Most students take the ACT for the first time during their junior year and repeat the test as seniors. Should you re-test? Statistically, re-testing results in an increase of a student's composite score 57% of the time; of the other 43% of re-testers, approximately half repeat their previous score and half do worse. But with the odds at least *somewhat* in your favor, a roomy limit of twelve attempts, and no obligation to share your potentially-lower score, it isn't the absolute worst idea.

But while the standard junior-senior plan is helpful, we'd like to reconsider desires for re-testing altogether; it is a long, mentally-taxing, 3- or 3½-hour event that costs $32 to $47, depending on the inclusion of the writing portion (though the event itself lasts closer to four hours, if you start the clock the moment you begin dealing with the formalities of checking in). Additionally, there are colleges whose sport programs require applicants to send each and every ACT score they receive; so, that fluke-score of 10 may be damaging to more than just your self-esteem. Therefore, instead of encouraging you to plan for re-testing, we prefer to negate that need altogether. *Or,* for the ambitious smarty pants out there, put your first score at 30-something and your second score at "Yes, yes, I would like a full-ride scholarship."

Sound good? Let's conjure up a plan!

CHAPTER 3

So, What's the Plan?

NOTES:

Let's start by seeing just how smart you really are! Prior to attacking any test-taking strategies, try a couple practice workouts for each subject to determine your strengths and weaknesses. If you have the TPS Workbook, there are several to choose from for each topic, with detailed answers and explanations in the back. This is a great tool to use in conjunction with this book. While you may want to just assume you'll do spiffy on the math portion, are you ready to bet your future on your assumed ability to multiply polynomials? Take a few minutes to find out where you truly stand; it'll help in developing an efficacious plan which, luckily for you, translates into less studying and more life beyond books.

STUDY ALL, NOT JUST WHERE YOU FALL

Hopefully, the assessment test has given you an idea of where you stand tall and where you fall short. As you develop your study-plan, aim to cover all four sections (or five, if you opt for the essay) sections in detail and spend extra time on any section in which you exhibit the most weakness. Again, don't avoid a subject simply because you think, "But I know this—why waste my time?" The correct answer: because one day you will want to be able to afford to put your own personal Moon Bounce in your backyard. (How awesome would *that* be?)

We know that it seems counterintuitive to dedicate your limited resources to a subject in which you feel confident, but it's also counterproductive to only carry a heavy burden with your weaker muscles when you have some serious strength in others. *Tone those which you've already built.* Additionally, studying information that builds on what you already know will be much more productive than stuffing your head with gibberish. And, as an added bonus, briefly studying a subject in which you are beyond proficient will provide a nice confidence boost to carry you through the tougher subjects.

STEPS IN DEVELOPING A PLAN

To help you make the most of your time, these steps will guide you through the development of a plan that is custom-tailored to your needs.

1. Determine how much time you have to study. If you only have three weeks until T-day, you're obviously going to need to move much faster than if you avoid procrastination and begin the process eight weeks prior to the big day. We recommend each student study for about 20 hours; how students allocate this time is determined by each individual's needs.

2. Try ranking subjects according to your perceived preparedness. (1 is the subject in which you feel most prepared and 5 is parenthesized for those not taking the writing portion.)

   1. _____   2. _____   3. _____
   4. _____   (5. _____)

NOTES:

3. Next, determine what percent of your time you think you should allocate to each section. If you did stellarly in reading but awfully in math, for example, you may need to allocate 10% of your time to reading and 30% to math. (But remember, while *you* can "give 110%," your time can only be given up to 100%.)

1. _____ 2. _____ 3. _____
4. _____ (5. _____)

4. Create a generic weekly study-plan. Keep the following in mind:

- If your plan is too ambitious, you may not be able to meet your goals. Instead of situating yourself for failure, be realistic. (If you've already scheduled your test date, this may equate to re-scheduling.)

- Find ways to reward yourself for your hard work. During this time of your life, it's likely that certain pleasures will have to be forgone; to fend off frustration, develop a simple reward system. For example, "If I complete eight half-hour sessions this week, I will go see a movie with friends." And no, you shouldn't take this book along. Take a break! (We know, it'll be hard. We *are* charming and all...)

WATCH
YOUR
WATCH

- Remember that you are a creature of habit and that certain habits will be difficult or even impossible to break. Don't assume you will be able to change your study habits or your love for a certain TV show. Instead, accept that you really can only study in 30-minute increments and that when "America's Next Biggest Idol" comes on, you turn into a certain root vegetable on the couch. Accept and accommodate.

- For those who enjoy study groups, determine why. Is it because others help fill-in the gaps of your knowledge, or is it because you receive the satisfaction of having participated in a study group without actually having to study? If you fit the first category, consider organizing intermittent sessions; however, bear in mind that most students achieve maximum efficiency by studying solo.

5. Decide which subject(s) will be addressed each day. Rotating back-and-forth between your worst subject and best subject will be more productive than focusing on one or the other for too long. This strategy will also allow your powerful subconscious

mind to process the new and/or difficult information
from your weaker subjects. Using the example
created in Step 2, list your subjects in the following
order: 1, 5, 2, 4, 3 (or, without the writing option: 1,
4, 3, 2). For example, if Joe's list looks like this:

1. Math _____   2. Science _____   3. English _____
4. Reading _____   5. Writing _____

   his rotation would look like this:

1. Math _____   5. Writing _____   2. Science _____
4. Reading _____   3. English _____

6. Create your typical schedule. Include school, work,
   extracurricular activities, "America's Next Biggest Idol",
   etc.

7. From step 3, assign realistic increments of time to
   each subject according to the amount of time per
   week you intend to study. Plug these ACT study
   times into your pre-existing schedule.

NOTES:

NOTES:

8. Once you have the time slots down, simplify the schedule to your ACT study-plan only.

9. Assign certain days or weeks to specific aspects of each subject.

10. Test your schedule and make alterations where necessary.

SAMPLE PLAN

This schedule is based on an April 9th testing date, during which time the student will be opting to take the writing portion of the ACT. The schedule begins February 13th, a full 8 weeks prior to the exam. Divvying up the 20 hours among 8, 5-day weeks, the student determined that (s)he must study an average of 2.5 hours per week, or 30 minutes per day. From steps 2 & 3 arose a weekly allocation:

1. Math – 15 minutes
2. Science – 30 minutes
3. Reading – 30 minutes
4. English – 30 minutes
5. Writing – 45 minutes

Applying the 1-5-2-4-3 rotation, assigning specific sections to study (e.g., Coordinate Geometry), and incorporating extra time for the subject that proves most difficult, the student can anticipate a schedule similar to this during his first four weeks of preparation:

Week	Sun	Mon	Tue	Wed	Thu	Fri	Sat
2/13	OFF	**M** intro 3-3:15	**W** intro 4-4:45	**S** intro 4-:4:30	**E** intro 6-6:30	**R** intro 3-3:30	OFF
2/20	**M** vocab 9-9:15	**W** scoring 3-3:45	**S** passage types 4-4:30	**E** components 4-4:30	**R** Q. types 6-6:30	OFF	OFF
2/27	**M** vocab 9-9:15 **W** plans 1-1:20	**S** reading 3-3:30	**E** punctuation 4-4:30	**R** Q. types 5-5:30	**W** plans 6-6:25	OFF	OFF
3/06	**M** pre-algebra 11-11:15	**W** writing well 3-3:45	OFF	**S** charts & graphs 4-4:30	**E** commas 6-6:30	**R** Q. types 3-3:30	OFF

Key: **E**nglish – **M**ath – **R**eading – **S**cience – **W**riting

As you work through the book, it may be helpful to track your progress from any practice tests that you take (additional practice tests can also be found online at www.ACT.org). Bi-weekly scoring will expose areas of deficit and provide an opportunity for you to rework your plan and refocus your energy on those weaker subjects. For those with experience in Excel or other spreadsheet programs, a subject- and composite-score presentation can be extremely helpful for a visual assessment of your

NOTES:

development; however, a simple pen-and-paper journal, as seen below, will suffice.

Assessment Date	Composite	English	Math	Reading	Science
Feb. 11	21	20	24	19	21
Feb. 18	21.5	20	25	20	21
Feb. 25	22.25	21	25	21	22
Mar. 4	23.75	23	26	22	24

For your convenience, we have supplied some blank charts in the back of this book so you can create your own schedule and track your practice test scores.

From the assessment test on February 11th to the first bi-weekly progress check, this student's composite score increased. However, the student's problematic area, Writing, did not change. Looking back at the schedule, the student began to dedicate extra time to this subject. By reassessing his or her ACT-preparedness, the student eliminated unproductive studying and focused on areas which increased his or her composite score more quickly.

A nice little byproduct of quickly, efficiently preparing for the ACT is the time you'll free up to do things like having a social life. But if you're more interested in technical literature than you are in fresh air or social outings, … well, maybe you should just skip this chapter and go straight to the next one where we'll coach you through the mental breakdown you're promised to experience.

CHAPTER 4

Enough with the Stress!

TEST PREP
SEMINARS

NOTES:

You've felt it all before:

rapid heartbeat,

clammy hands,

sporadic and distracting thoughts,

tension headaches

— and the ailments go on and on. While the rush of adrenaline may have been beneficial back in our flee from saber-toothed tiger days, it's crippling now that we're trying to complete complex mental tasks. Those devious ACT creators are counting on this negative stress to break you!

Now for some advice from Doctor Test Prep: normal levels of stress are good—they encourage us to perform at our peaks by creating immediate resource reserves—but when we're sitting still to study, those resources go unused. This excess energy causes chronic stress and all of those bonuses disappear under a wave of debilitating symptoms.

Here's an epiphany for you: no one is impressed with your frantic study schedule that leaves you sleep deprived. Not only is expending energy on high levels of stress uncomfortable and frustrating, but it's also counterproductive. It makes concentrating difficult, it impairs judgment, and it causes snags during the memory storage and recall processes. And, worst of all, it's a vicious, downward spiral of ever-increasing anxiety.

The bottom line is this: stop stressing! Identify and address the causes of your negative stress. Are you not sticking to your study plan? Reschedule it. Do you feel hopeless in a specific subject? Dedicate more time to it. Are you just not getting enough sleep? Forgo that hour of television before bed. Whatever the issue, the only way to deal with stress is to confront the problem. Until resolved, however, there are certain techniques that help manage stress.

NOTES:

STRESS DETERENCE TIPS & TECHNIQUES

As sincere as your attempt to be hyper-organized and efficient in this journey may be, it's understandable (if not expected) for you to become a little flustered or anxious. If properly handled, however, the budding of high stress levels doesn't have to be detrimental. Try the following on for size:

☑ Look in the mirror for 30 seconds. Really. Be straight with yourself. The more you try to convince yourself that your anxieties aren't valid, the more detrimental they'll become. Instead of denying yourself the right to be anxious, honestly address the root of your distress and make positive lifestyle changes.

☑ Maintain an optimistic viewpoint throughout all aspects of your life. The more positive you are as a whole, the more support you will be able to offer yourself during hours of frustration. Additionally, if you are able to optimistically envision yourself waltzing in on exam day and casually showing the test who's boss, you're walking the same path as many of the most successful business people in the world who live by the motto "visualize, then actualize." You don't have to do the hippie dance on the quad; you can simply change your attitude internally.

☑ Eliminate the fear of a shocking surprise by acknowledging that the ACT is predictable and that you have a road-map to it in your hands. Just know what you need to know!

☑ Normalize ACT test-taking through the establishment of a routine in an efficient, comfortable setting. Avoid distracting, cramped, cluttered rooms; create a setting of productivity. If this means turning off the soap opera that is your cell phone, do it. You can always catch up on the drama when you're done with your study session.

SCORES→

Anxiety→

AND ONCE YOU'RE HIGH-STRUNG ...

Stress-aversion techniques aren't exactly bulletproof (as we're sure you'll notice), so it's best to arm yourself with methods that fight the effects of anxiety and tension as they develop. The following methods require no tools other than your willingness and are sit-in-seat friendly.

☑ Remember when you used to terrify your little sister by moving your scalp around as if it were detached? Well, that little trick can actually relieve some of the tension we accumulate on a daily basis. Slide your hands across your scalp, into a section of your hair and squeeze the sides of your fingers together so that they're parallel. Maintaining this grasp, slowly pull the hair away from your scalp in successive tugs, pulling only as strongly as feels pleasant to you.

☑ Give your poor eyes a break! Close your eyes and casually roll them in alternating circles to give the muscles a little stretch. Once they've loosened a little, cross them and look up, and then down, as far as possible. Uncross them and cover your eye sockets with cupped hands to block out the light for about fifteen seconds. If you feel the potential for a tension headache, dedicate even more time to the last step—it'll be well worth the time, *especially* if you're in the middle of the real test.

☑ Allow your head to laze toward any one direction until you are no longer providing it support. Slowly rotate your head in a clockwise fashion, followed by counter-clockwise. Never push any muscle to stretch; if it isn't pliable, stretching it too far will only cause discomfort. Also try closing your eyes tightly and turning your head to the far right and far left, using a rotation of your hips to keep your eyes generally faced forward and out of suspicious trying-to-catch-a-glimpse-of-another-exam territory (your proctor *will* be watching for such behavior).

Neck Rolls

☑ Sitting up straight with your arms at your sides, push your shoulders back and feel the stretch through your chest. Roll your shoulders toward your ears and then forward until you feel hunched. Finish by pushing your mid-back forward, your shoulders backward, and your spine into a curve.

☑ Attempt to momentarily "pause" all thoughts and perform a few sigh breaths: slowly breathe inward through your nose until your diaphragm pushes your stomach outward. Paying close attention to your muscles as they loosen, release a lengthy exhale until your lungs feel empty. Take the time to experience the feeling of emptiness before repeating an inhale.

☑ Extend your hands at your sides and shake them vigorously. This will help with writer's cramp and with expending the excess energy you'll inevitably build up as you sit still.

☑ Lift your feet from the floor, straighten your legs, and rotate your ankles. Pushing your heels forward with your toes facing upward can also do wonders for a tense hamstring.

"Wait," you object, "I won't do those silly exercises in public!" Oh, really? Before you decide that you're more than willing to utilize these de-stressing methods at home but *never, ever in public*, consider your options: drop another $32 to $47 on a re-test and waste the many hours you've dedicated to studying, or recognize that everyone around you is just as hyper-focused on his own test as you are and, thus will never notice your

movements. Don't be silly: do whatever seated dance you need in order to succeed! The ACT is not a fashion show and we give you special dispensation for acting like a study geek while in the test. (This license is not valid, however, outside the testing site.)

OK, our turn to be the nagging parent:

YOU NEED A GOOD DIET, EXERCISE, AND SUFFICIENT SLEEP!

NAG

Sorry, but it's true. One of the best ways to battle elevated levels of stress is to make strides toward establishing a healthy diet, exercise routine, and sleep schedule. Building resilience against stress's effects by promoting a healthy mind and body allows you to focus all of your energy on the task at hand. Unfortunately, many of these tasks have been made difficult—though far from impossible—by the modern lifestyle.

NAG: Put down that "dollar menu" burger and listen up! We get it…properly feeding oneself can be quite an inconvenient chore. While we can easily grab a frozen burrito or bag of chips, the task of maintaining our health is much more daunting. Ready-made snacks and foods are often high in sugars and saturated fats and extremely low in the nutrients our bodies crave. Give your body a high-five and ditch on-the-go foods such as candy bars, soda pop, potato chips, fried foods, etc. While these snacks may give you a little jolt at first, they'll definitely send you crashing into a rut worse than before. So opt for foods high in protein, which keep you energized, and fiber, which keeps your tummy satisfied and not pregnant with a grizzly bear. It is also important to keep your body properly hydrated, so drink plenty of water and steer clear of coffee. Coffee is a go-to favorite of the nervous and the exhausted, but it's a natural diuretic (which you may begin to regret half-way into the exam!) and can do more harm than good. And beware of highly-caffeinated energy drinks; they are notorious for amping you up and then letting you drop like a lead balloon.

NAG

NAG: Regular exercise accomplishes a plethora of positives, and the more you work through the initial blockade of laziness, the more easily you will be able to ignore those couch-potato pangs. Additionally, exercise helps expend the excess energy and tension we accumulate while sitting still to study, consequently making both studying and sleeping at the end of the night much easier.

NAG: And regarding sleep: it is extremely important! (We know…why aren't you hearing this from Mom or Dad on Saturday morning? Use this one next time… you're welcome by the way!) We have all been told how important slumber is for our bodies and mental clarity, but recent studies have solidified the power of the unconscious mind. As we sleep, our brains reorganize and repeatedly analyze the information we've learned during the day; without any effort, we digest this new material and assimilate it into our repertoire. So while you don't see the need for that extra hour of sleep, consider what good it could do for you. Try it for a couple days and assess that extra hour's benefits.

NAG: Maintaining a healthy lifestyle is important in all aspects of your life; if you have not yet developed a plan to achieve a healthy balance, now is the time to take it into consideration. For more information regarding physical wellness, we recommend speaking with your physician or school counselor; both will have a mountain of resources to start you off on your way toward wellness.

So once all our nagging and life and sleep modification advice turns your life around, eliminates those dark circles under your eyes so you get more attention from that cute guy/girl, and you become deliriously happy and very wealthy one day, don't forget about us here over at Test Prep Seminars!

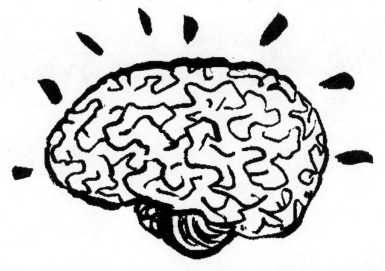

NOTES:

CHAPTER 5

The Dreaded Test Day

Prepare your gray matter for the exam all you please, but if you don't know some of the mundane basics—location, timing, acceptable gear, etc.—your day probably won't go quite as well as you'd like. As inconsequential as five minutes may sound, just three-hundred seconds could spell disaster for your exam day.

LOCATION & TIME

Every second of your testing period follows a very strict schedule. According to the proctors and other test-takers, arriving late is not acceptable, regardless of any (un)foreseen circumstance. After all, would you appreciate your 8 weeks of hard work being jeopardized by a tardy peer stumbling in the door? Doubt it. It's extremely important that you know the exact location and time of your exam, and preferably that you know this information days ahead of time. Furthermore, you should be familiar with the route and travel time in order to accurately gauge a safe departure-time on the big day.

WHAT TO BRING – AND WHAT DEFINITELY <u>NOT</u> TO BRING

Many of these points seem pretty obvious, but how many times have you suddenly realized how well you fit into that Space Cadet uniform? We're not always on our game - such as when we're a tidbit nervous about an exam that essentially tells the school of your dreams whether you're an A+ at baking brownies or an A+ at academics - so take a moment to consider these points and develop your own test-day check list.

Mirror, mirror, out in space, who has the best looking face?

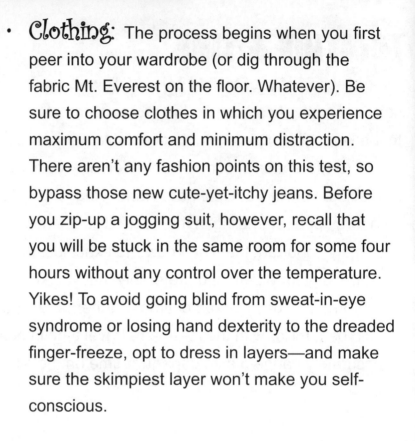

- **Clothing:** The process begins when you first peer into your wardrobe (or dig through the fabric Mt. Everest on the floor. Whatever). Be sure to choose clothes in which you experience maximum comfort and minimum distraction. There aren't any fashion points on this test, so bypass those new cute-yet-itchy jeans. Before you zip-up a jogging suit, however, recall that you will be stuck in the same room for some four hours without any control over the temperature. Yikes! To avoid going blind from sweat-in-eye syndrome or losing hand dexterity to the dreaded finger-freeze, opt to dress in layers—and make sure the skimpiest layer won't make you self-conscious.

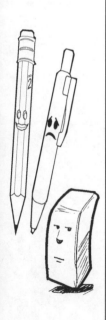

- **Pencils and Erasers:** We all have our favorite writing utensil, but when you're taking the ACT, it's time to embrace the old-fashioned #2. Not only can mechanical pencils be more time-consuming and difficult to erase, but they're not even permitted. You should also bring more ready-to-use pencils than you think you'll ever need and only have a sharpener for the freak event that you manage to break a pencil on every other page of the test. Additionally, bring a couple of your favorite erasers. While you're obviously not going to kill an entire bar eraser in one sitting, you may accidentally knock it off your desk and watch it bounce majestically to the other side of the room. But hey, you have two more (right?), so you'll just grab it later.

- **Snacks and Beverages:** You're not going to have a lunch break, but there *is* a ten-minute break between the math and reading sections, and a nutritious snack can do wonders for your concentration. Pack a treat that is low in sugar and high in longer-term energy; omit the candy bar and pack a mixed bag of rolled granola, your favorite nuts, and a small amount of dried fruit (the naturally high sugar content of fruit has potential to make you crash after a short burst of energy, so munch lightly). As for beverages, your body loves water best! Alternatively, if you're a fan of sports drinks, check the sugar content on the nutrition label; they're often much more sugary than you'd expect. And if you're a soda-lover, get over it. Sugar and carbonation are not your friends today. Lastly, don't go "wanderer-in-the-desert" on your Big Gulp beverage and torture your desk with two hours of your sitting rendition of the potty-dance.

- **Calculator:** You and your calculator should be well-acquainted and understand each other when you say, "Cosecant, please!" or when it replies, "ERROR UNDEFINED." Mid-ACT is simply *not* the time to learn the function of the [$^{-1}$] key. Oh, also, registration isn't the time to learn that the calculator you've become BFF with isn't allowed. For the most up-to-date list of prohibited calculators, visit www.act.org and search the term "calculators."

- **Photo I.D.:** Even if you've spent years getting buddy-buddy with the nerdiest kid on your block, you can't hire him to take the ACT on your behalf. The check-in process necessitates an official form of photographic identification: school I.D., passport, state I.D., driver's license, etc. If you don't own any of these and cannot obtain one, your other option is to shake down your school for a letter of identification. (Check your ACT registration book for details.)

- **Admission Ticket:** You should receive this via snail mail some two weeks prior to the big day. Integrate your admission ticket into your test-day kit and do not remove it until it is being handed over to one of the proctors. If you *happen* to misplace your admission ticket for some strange and inexplicable reason (definitely not because it became the final resting place of your chewed gum), give the ACT a ring at (319) 337-1270. You also can print off the ticket online.

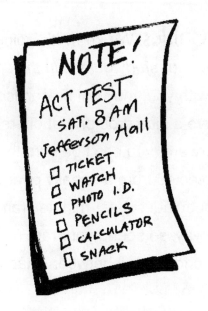

NOTES:

Devices

Don't TRY IT!

Now that you have what you need, let's cover some of the things you don't need:

- **Study Guides:** We know it's going to be hard, *but leave your study guides in the car!* If you bring them in with you, they will be confiscated. Even if you have a nice proctor that offers to hold them until afterward, you can't be sure they'll have been protected from a sneaky peer or from your own forgetfulness. Last-minute cramming doesn't help anyway, so spend your rare moments of freedom prior to and between exams seeking inner peace.

- **Your Cell phone:** Distance makes the heart grow fonder, so spend a second apart from your latest crush's cutesy texts and leave your phone in the car. Plus, do you want to risk forgetting to silence the ringtone? Even if it's on vibrate, there's no guarantee it won't make the keys in your pocket resonate a tune which instantly evokes violent rage from your peers. This goes for all electronics: leave them behind; they're not allowed.

  Please note: If you do find yourself going through Device Withdrawal Symptoms in just four hours, it is possible that you do have a device problem. Seek help.

- **Blank Paper:** It's simply too easy to make an undetectable cheat-sheet and pass it off as scratch paper. The ACT council recognizes this, and thus they say, "No." Your booklet will have sufficient blank space to do your work so don't sweat it.

YOUR PEERS AND PROCTORS

You aren't at this event to make friends and neither is anyone else. Do not be disturbed by others' sharpness or coldness—they're probably just as nervous and hyper-focused as you. Even so, you should be too preoccupied with that inner peace task to notice their grumpy mugs. As far as your peers go, your only obligation is to be conscientious. Now is a good time to practice that cold, aloof alter ego. You can resume being your bubbly, people-pleasing self in a few hours.

As for the ACT proctors, they are there to do a job—and a very serious job at that. They will be well-versed in what is and isn't acceptable; don't bicker with them at any point—you won't win. Listen attentively to your guides and be mindful of their directives.

Whatever you do, don't let last-minute details prove fatal to your hard work. Pull a Santa: make a list and check it twice (or thrice, or perhaps frice? Frice isn't a word, but "four times" ruins the flow).

PROCTOR

CHAPTER 6

A Test of Your Time Management Skills

NOTES:

The ACT is an assessment of much more than your college-readiness; by packing 215 questions into 175 minutes, it is also an acute evaluation of your endurance and time management skills. ACT writers are very tricky; don't trust them. Their evil *Time Panic* torture device may turn your testing peers into jello, but you know better! This section is applicable to all portions of the test, so you may want to pay extra-close attention to the following test-taking strategies.

- That watch we talked about earlier? You better bring it. Knowing how much time you have to budget will allow you to better do so. Just make sure you've disabled all alarms. If your watch makes any sounds, you will be dismissed from the exam and your sheet will go unscored. (And no, you can't get a refund.)

- Have section-ending times written on the front page of your test booklet. If you forget an end-time, you won't have to think too hard—just flip the pages back and take a glance.

- Complete the questions of an entire page in the booklet itself prior to transferring your answers to the bubble sheet. Repeatedly reorienting yourself in a world of ambiguous bubbles can be surprisingly time-consuming.

- Your pencil should *never* leave your hand. Even if you just fiddle with it, a pencil in hand is much more accessible than a pencil on the table.

- Sometimes guessing is the best option. If you find yourself hung up on a specific question, avoid the speed bump; make an educated guess and move on. If you foresee spare time, circle the problem in your test booklet and return later to re-evaluate—but don't leave the question without an answer (yes, even if it's a stab in the dark), just in case you don't make it around to a second sweep of the page.

NOTES:

- If an answer isn't obvious, deal with the question by eliminating bad answers. ~~Strike them out~~ so you don't waste time re-reading or reconsidering answers you know to be incorrect. The fewer possible answers you are left to choose from, the higher your probability of choosing correctly.

- <u>Underlining</u> information in a question or passage can be extremely helpful for two reasons: 1. you can quickly relocate important information, and 2. you will be reading more *actively*, thus paying more attention and absorbing more information.

- If you identify a question as vastly more complex than you feel capable of handling, or if you're in the midst of the math section and foresee spending well over the 60 second-per-question mark on this *one* point, it's time for an educated guess. All questions are worth the same number of points, so you might as well get two easy questions done instead of that one hard one. (Trust us, if you only score a 15, no one will be impressed—or even believe—that you managed to solve the hardest question on the test.)

Tips

- Take the briefest of brief notes in the margin as you read. A single word marker can function as a beacon of hope amid a large, scary sea of words. Instead of having to re-read the whole paragraph for that one concept, you can simply locate your scribble.

- Decode the alien language test-writers love to exploit: restate the question in your native tongue and *then* try to formulate your answer.

- And one of the easiest things you can do: memorize the directions before test-day! At the beginning of each subject's chapter in this book will be the instructions; pay very close attention to them and re-read them each time you open that chapter until you know them as well as you know the lyrics to your favorite song.

Speaking of managing your time well, why don't we get started right away? Turn the page!

CHAPTER 7

English

Welcome to the wonderful world of the English language!

Student: meet the English Language.

English Language: meet the student.

Don't be fretful—she's just as afraid of you as you are of her—and rightfully so. Can you imagine what it must feel like to be verbally abused on a daily basis?

Texting, Chirping, 1337 speak, fo'shizzling

...let's just say: English has officially

entered counseling.

And you? You just have to deal with the ACT English section. (How lucky!)

In 45 minutes, you will read five pieces of prose and answer 75 questions; 40 questions will concern usage and mechanics while 35 questions will concern rhetorical skills. Usage and mechanics cover adverb vs. adjective, subject-verb agreement, pronoun usage, verb tense, parallelism, punctuation, and sentence fragments. (Don't be afraid of these scary words, they're harmless.) Rhetorical skills cover overall organization, proper use of transitions, idea clarity, precision and redundancy, and theme and voice. (Again, harmless.)

The upcoming lessons should function as an anchor and a preface to future reading sessions. The most effective way to study for the English portion of the ACT is through exposure to the rules followed by attentive reading; whether your pieces of choice are authored by your favorite contemporary novelist or a classical writer, your attention to their adherence to these rules is the key to your success.

NOTES:

memorize the
DIRECTIONS

Begin the adventure by reading the official ACT directions:

Directions: *In the following five passages, certain words and phrases have been underlined and numbered. You will find alternatives for each underlined portion in the right-hand column. Select the one that best expresses the idea, that makes the statement acceptable in standard written English, or that is phrased most consistently with the style and tone of the entire passage. If you feel that the original version is best, select "NO CHANGE." You will also find questions asking about a section of the passage or about the entire passage.*

For these questions decide which choice gives the most appropriate response to the given question. For each question in the test, select the best choice and fill in the corresponding space on the answer folder. You may wish to read each passage through before you begin to answer the questions associated with it. Most answers cannot be determined without reading several sentences around the phrases in question. Make sure to read far enough ahead each time you choose an alternative.

While this text will be using some of the scary terminology you're surely dreading, what is important is that you normalize the rules themselves, not the terminology. The ACT will not ask you why a prepositional phrase doesn't affect subject-verb agreement, but it may expect you to know when it is grammatically correct to have "butterflies is" in your sentence. (Psst, it's acceptable if *the wave of butterflies is coming, run!*)

COMPONENTS OF LANGUAGE

Knowing the different parts of speech was extremely helpful in deciphering those nasty little DOU's our elementary school teachers gave us back in the day (daily oral usage tests, in case you're one of the few who've been able to forget the pain). Lucky us, it's also going to be helpful now! Take a moment and make sure you have a pretty good understanding of the vocabulary below. As mentioned before, you won't need to regurgitate this information on the ACT, but having a good handle on the components of language will help us discuss the rules you *will* need to know.

DOUs

Noun – Person, place, thing, or concept
   » Alexander, cat, firetruck, hometown, chemistry

Pronoun – Stand-in for a noun where it would otherwise be repeated
   » Him, it, me, she, they, us, we, you

NOTES:

Adjective – Modifier of a (pro)noun

> » Aloof, dull, fabulous, quirky, slimy, watchful

Verb – Identification of an action

> » Bury, enjoy, jostle, nag, yawn

Adverb – Description/modification of a verb, adjective, or another adverb

> » Angrily, blissfully, lazily, ravenously

Helping/Auxiliary Verb – Alters the tense of a main verb

> » I _could_ be rocking out to Justin Bieber if I weren't so ashamed; but, alas, I am.

Preposition – Description of the relationship between two pieces of a sentence

> » We dance, we dance, we dance _around_ the Mexican hat.

Subject – A noun which is performing an action

> » _Jane_ called her best friend.

Predicate – The action which the subject is performing. Predicates and verbs may seem like the same thing, namely an action, but they are different in that the predicate elaborates beyond the verb and says something extra about the subject. The following examples have the (verb in parenthesis) and the _predicate underlined and italicized_.

» The kitten (_meowed_) _profusely_.

» Juan (_saw_) _the firework display on Independence Day with Sue._

» My friends and I (_love_) _to go for jogs along the lake_.

GOT THAT?

Direct Object – The recipient of the predicate

» Becky requested a _vacation_.

Indirect Object – The recipient of the direct object

» Lightning filled the sky, which gave _the children_ a light show.

Compound Sentence – Fusion of two independent clauses in one sentence through the use of a conjunction

» Always be prepared _and_ always remember pants.

Coordinating Conjunction – Connector of words or groups of words that are of equal importance

» Life gave us lemons _but_ no sugar.

Coordinating conjunctions can be memorized with a neat little mnemonic:

FANBOYS

For,

And,

Nor,

But,

Or,

Yet,

So.

Subordinating Conjunction – Connector of two clauses to form complex sentences

» I'd prefer to see a double <u>rather</u> than a single rainbow.

Comma Splices – Also known as run-on sentences, an incorrectly punctuated compound sentence

» The book is <u>heavy, I</u> don't like heavy books.

The segments before and after the comma are both complete sentences; while they may be conjoined as a compound sentence, there is no conjunction to complete the process.

NOTES:

Clause – An expression containing a <u>*subject*</u> and *predicate*

» That <u>*monkey*</u> just threw *poop*!

Independent Clause – Also known as a *main clause*, an independent clause is an expression of a complete thought (complete sentence). An independent clause is different from a complete sentence only in that an independent clause can exist without punctuation whereas a complete sentence requires punctuation.

» <u>*She never heard him coming*</u>.

(Notice the period is not underlined as part of the independent clause.)

Dependent Clause – Expression of an incomplete thought (not a complete sentence). Dependent clauses are often identified via a *dependent word marker* such as *after, although, as (if), because, before, since, though, unless, whatever, while*, et cetera.

» Because he was a ninja.

(What is/occurs because he is a ninja?)

sneaking in late again?

If a dependent clause exists independently of a main clause, we have a *sentence fragment* on our hands.

NOTES:

GOT
THAT?

Phrase – A group of words that doesn't contain both a subject and a predicate

» In the barn. (Who/what is in the barn?)

Preposition – Links nouns, pronouns, and phrases to other parts of a sentence.

» Witches love to ride brooms <u>over</u> the townspeople

Prepositional Phrase – Description of relationship between a (pro)noun and another word

» At home, by herself, from swimming, with me

Prepositional Idioms – Generally accepted preposition combinations which do not follow any general sort of rule

» Concerned with, grateful for, put up with, prior to

Modifier – Words, phrases, or clauses that provide a more accurate description of a word

» <u>After the argument</u>, they decided to part ways.

Dangling Modifier – A misplaced modifier that focuses on a word other than that which was intended.

» <u>Falling off the bed</u>, Anne caught the small child.

(Who is falling?)

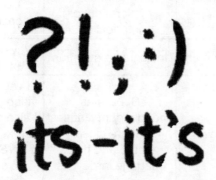

PUNCTUATION

We know you've been using basic punctuation for years, but do you remember the usage rules for those less commonly encountered, such as the dash and the semicolon? (The latter of which happens to be one of the most effective punctuation tools in writing; if you're doing the writing portion of the ACT, we highly recommend you practice using them.)

NOTES:

Symbol	Name	Uses	Example
.	period	Ends a sentence	Giraffes are funny looking.
!	exclamation point	Ends a command, emphatic declaration, or interjection	Chill out! I love cupcakes! Stop interrupting me!
?	question mark	Indicates a question	Why do my feet smell like oatmeal cookies?
;	semicolon	Separates independent clauses that are closely related and helps manage large lists	I want to buy a new video game; however, I also don't want to be broke this weekend. *(See Comma examples on the following pages.)*
:	colon	Introduces a list following an independent clause and separates independent clauses from quotations	If you're allergic to peanuts, you can expect the following from these cookies: itchiness, wheezing, and serious cramps. Nancy made a fantastic suggestion: "We should play four square!"
-	hyphen	Creates compound words and ideas, spells out numbers 21 through 99 and fractions, adds *some* prefixes, and allows for shortening lists with the same ending	Don't drive the wrong way down a one-way street; if you get pulled over, you can kiss your all-inclusive Spring Break vacation goodbye! I babysat children who were one-, two-, and six-years old.
" "	quotation marks	Signifies quoted or spoken information as well as titles of articles, poems, and short stories	She asked me, "Wait, why did you put a lollipop in your nose?" I loved the piece "How to Bathe a Broom."

NOTES:

Symbol	Name	Uses	Example
—	dash	Sets off parenthetical information; always use in pairs unless the information comes at the end of the sentence	Her many animals—including a tiger and a monkey—were treated extremely well. Her hair started on fire—she probably shouldn't have gotten that close to the candle.
( )	parenthesis	Marks the inclusion of information which the author does not find as important as the rest of the sentence	The strangest thing about our journey to Chicago was the complete lack of shoes on our feet on the way home (don't ask; we don't know).
'	apostrophe	Creates contractions[†] and possessive forms[‡]	Don't mess-up Samantha's hair; she'll freak!

[†] One of the quickest ways to lose points in this section is confusing "it's" with "its." Read this carefully and make it your own: "It's" is a contraction for "it is" and "its" is the possessive form of "it." Furthermore, "*its'*," with an apostrophe after the S, *is not a real word*.

[‡] For possessive forms, the apostrophe comes between the (pro)noun and the possessive S (e.g. the dog's collar) unless the (pro)noun is made plural via an S, in which case the apostrophe comes after the plural S (e.g. the dogs' collars, indicating multiple dogs owning collars).

COMMAS

Last, but *far* from least, is the comma. Since the comma is the most frequently used (and thereby most frequently misused) form of punctuation, we're separating it from the main list in order to provide in-depth explanations of proper usage.

(1) Separation of two independent clauses. You must use a conjunction to link the two clauses together.

1. We love tans, but we hate cancer more.
2. The camera does not shoot in black and white, nor does it shoot in sepia.
3. Would you like to come, or do you have other plans?

(2) Separation of items in a series.

1. Eat well, sleep well, and expect to do well.
2. I always start my day with a coffee, a run and a shower.
3. The kids spent all day learning, creating and chasing.

(3) Separation of introductory clauses, phrases, or words.

1. If you are a vegetarian, this pot roast is not for you.
2. Studying all day, she forgot to do laundry.
3. However, her new perfume smells delightful.

(4) Isolation of phrases and words nonessential to the main idea expressed in a sentence. (We've *italicized* nonessential phrases and words; note that the removal of the italicized information leaves behind a complete sentence.)

1. Jane, *the best cook in our group*, surprised us when she admitted to using play dough in her cupcakes.
2. The plane, *battered by the storm*, was forced to land.
3. Fluffy, *as much as we love the itty, bitty, kitty committee*, must be spayed.

Take care not to isolate information essential to the expression of the main idea. Take the following for example:

> The child who won this year's Spelling Bee wasn't taught any English until she was six years-old!

Here we wouldn't isolate "who won this year's Spelling Bee" via commas because it is essential to the the main idea. Without the clarification, it's impossible to see why it is of any importance that the child is new to the English language.

(5) Separation of coordinate adjectives (i.e. adjectives which modify the same word); use only if the idea remains intact when "and" is used in place of the comma.

1. Our warm, home-cooked dinner was delicious.
2. Our hasty, ill-conceived stunt didn't work very well.
3. Yesterday's mood was set by a gloomy, overcast sky.

(6) Introduction and isolation of a quotation.

1. "That material is absolutely gorgeous," Anne remarked.
2. Shakespeare wrote, "Frailty, thy name is woman!"
3. As much as I begged, the teacher bluntly replied, "No."

(7) Isolation of addresses, dates, numbers, and proper titles.

1. August 13, 2009, was the best day of my life.
2. How can I find 2190 Constance Ave., Racine, WI?
3. Please refer to George Stone, Ph.D., for advice.

(8) Separation of direct addresses, interjections, and transitional phrases.

1. *Mother*, will you teach me how to multiply?
2. That, *my dear*, is how one aces the ACT!
3. I would, *therefore*, like to visit Spain promptly.

(9) Isolation of parenthetical elements non-essential, though considered equally important, to the sentence as a whole. Sentence remains intact even if information is omitted.

1. Dress pants and skirts, *not jeans*, are expected.
2. My fingernails, *frequently polished*, are quite healthy.
3. The printer, *clunky and dusty*, only works intermittently.

Did you already know all of these rules? Oh, really? Move on to the next sub-section and prove it.

USAGE AND MECHANICS

Here we will cover the most commonly tested aspects of proper writing. On the next two pages, incorrect sentences are presented. First read the incorrect versions two or three times each and try to determine the errors. Initially, we recommend that you read sentences out loud to actually hear the correct and erroneous versions of the examples—after all, you listen to spoken language *all* the time, whereas you likely only *read* a small fraction of that time. As you read, record your thoughts on a separate piece of paper. Once you have a suspect in mind for each grammatical/structural crime, turn the page for a detailed explanation.

NOTES:

As you compare notes, please keep in mind that language is an art form. Consider the outcome if you asked ten people to produce the color of an apple: seven would show different variations of red, two would show green apples and one might be yellow. Language has the same intricacies; a sentence can be constructed in an astonishing number of different and yet equally valid ways.

So does anything look "weird" here???

Find the crime in each of the following sentences.

1. I love to bite into a freshly picked orange the only ones we have are refrigerated.
2. My favorite activities are to run, to read fiction, and swimming.
3. To who does this belong?
4. Each of the children said a somber goodbye to the teacher as they walked out the classroom and into summer vacation.
5. We were forced to listen to that song every day, it was still our favorite.
6. This blueberry muffin is the tastiest of the two.
7. As she filed paperwork, a giant spider caught Megan's eye.

8. If they ever decide to pack up and go home.

9. Us had a great time at the bowling alley.

10. She spoke to the children very nice.

11. All of the cats has a personal food dish.

12. If we all show fewer attention to our own happiness and more attention to the basic needs of others, less people will starve on the streets of the richest nation on the planet.

13. Part-time jobs help students in their early teens develop fiscal constraint by learning the true value of money, social responsibility by adhering to a strict schedule and being obedient to management, and learning to take pride from a hard day of work.

14. They're car is entirely too small to fit all of the band equipment.

15. I have two siblings—Jack and Steven—but he is taller.

16. The viewers were deeply effected by the whaling video footage.

17. It is of utmost importance that you adhere with the rules!

While you probably noticed that *something* was wrong with each of the sentences, were you able to identify *and* remedy the problem? Here are the corrections and an explanation of the grammatical or structural error. (And remember the apple!)

(1) I love to bite into a freshly picked orange the only ones we have are refrigerated.

Run-on Sentences *occur when two independent clauses are conjoined without proper punctuation or when too much information is presented in a single sentence. For this example, a backslash separates the two clauses:*

> I love to bite into a freshly picked orange / the only ones we have are refrigerated.

This sentence can be corrected with a conjunction and a comma:

> I love to bite into a freshly picked orange, but the only ones we have are refrigerated.

Or with a semicolon and an adverb:

> I love to bite into a freshly picked orange; however, the only ones we have are refrigerated.

NOTES:

The latter form of a run-on (in which too much information is relayed in a single sentence) is exemplified by the following:

> Eric still hasn't called his grandmother to wish her a belated "Happy Birthday," he'd forgotten to call the day before due to a horrendously over-booked schedule, and now he can't bear to face her.

As you can see, the sentence contains too much information and slowly loses the reader. To correct this example, either a semicolon or a period should follow "belated 'Happy Birthday:'"

> Eric still hasn't called his grandmother to wish her a belated "Happy Birthday;" he'd forgotten to call the day before due to a horrendously over-booked schedule, and now he can't bear to face her.

or

> Eric still hasn't called his grandmother to wish her a belated "Happy Birthday." He'd forgotten to call the day before due to a horrendously over-booked schedule, and now he can't bear to face her.

NOTES:

(2) My favorite activities are to run, to read fiction, and swimming.

Verb Parallelism refers to the use of the same verb form in a list. If the list begins with a gerund form of a verb (e.g. joking), the consequent main verbs must also follow the gerund form. The problem in our example is "swimming" because the two previous verbs were infinitive verbs; the correct sentence is:

> My favorite activities are to run, to read fiction and to swim.

NOTES:

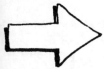

(3) To who does this belong?

Who versus Whom is one of the most difficult distinctions for students to make. Both are pronouns, but who is the subject of a sentence and whom is the object of a sentence. If this doesn't clarify the issue for you, brush up on subject and object before proceeding to (4).

Another trick, however, is to turn your who(m) issue into a "masculine" question: "Who(m) just ruffled my hair?" Which sounds correct, "Him ruffled my hair," or, "He ruffled my hair"? The latter—the one without an "m"— makes most sense, so the question would be "Who just ruffled my hair?" Consider sentence (3) above:

"To who(m) does this belong?"

Your response would be, "It belongs to him," not, "It belongs to he." Notice the correct answer has an "m" whereas the incorrect does not; hence, in this situation, the correct question to ask is:

"To whom does this belong?"

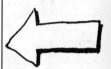

(4) Each of the children said a somber goodbye to the teacher as they walked out the classroom and into summer vacation.

Pronoun-Noun Plurality Agreement *refers to a noun and a pronoun having the same plurality. This example is probably one of the trickiest you will see because of the sneaky "each" at the beginning. While "children" is plural, "each" is singular and therefore dictates that the pronoun must be singular. Hence, "they" is incorrect and our sentence should be:*

> Each of the children said a somber goodbye to the teacher as *he or she* walked out of the classroom and into summer vacation.

NOTES:

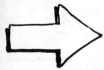

(5) We were forced to listen to that song every day, it was still our favorite.

Comma Splices *occur when two independent clauses are merged into one sentence solely through the use of a comma. Comma splices can be remedied in many ways: a conjunction can be added, a semicolon can be utilized, or the clauses can be separated altogether via a period. Our incorrect sentence can be remedied the following ways:*

> We were forced to listen to that song every day, yet it was still our favorite.

or

> We were forced to listen to that song every day; however, it was still our favorite.

or

> We were forced to listen to that song every day. It was still our favorite.

NOTES:

(6) This blueberry muffin is the tastiest of the two.

-Er and -est *are used when comparing two items and when comparing three or more items, respectively. This example misuses -est when only two items are being assessed. The correction is as follows:*

This blueberry muffin is the tastier of the two.

*The same goes for **more/most** and **between/among**. More and between are used when comparing two items (or two major groups of items); Most and among are used when comparing three or more things (additionally, among can be used when the number of items is unknown).*

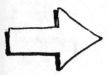

(7) As she filed paperwork, a giant spider caught Megan's eye.

Misplaced Modifiers occur when a modifier is placed in a sentence so that it clarifies incorrectly. In this example, "As she filed paperwork" is our modifier and "Megan" is the subject. Unfortunately, as written, our sentence declares that a giant, paperwork-filing spider reaches out and grabs Megan's eyeball. What was actually meant follows:

As she filed paperwork, Megan's eye caught a glimpse of a giant spider.

*The "trick" is to read sentences on a literal level; if your mind didn't rearrange the thoughts because you **know** spiders don't file paperwork, how would you interpret the sentence?*

NOTES:

(8) If they ever decide to pack up and go home.

Fragments *occur when a dependent clause tries to assert its autonomy by hanging out all alone. If you're privy to what makes a complete sentence, however, you'll quickly recognize when there isn't a subject, a verb, or a complete thought present. Additionally, finding fragments is particularly easy since the question will refer to a portion of the passage which contains a period. If this is the case, be skeptical of the sentence. But back to our example: we clearly do not have a complete thought. "If they ever decide to pack up and go home," then what? Well, it could be anything, really, which is exactly why it is an incomplete idea.*

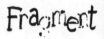

If they ever decide to pack up and go home, we can finally get some rest.

If they ever decide to pack up and go home, I can stop pretending to study!

(But really—stop pretending.)

NOTES:

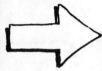

(9) Us had a great time at the bowling alley.

Object versus Subject Pronoun *confusion occurs when a pronoun replaces an object or a subject but the incorrect form of the pronoun is used. For example, him (object) and he (subject) are often confused. In our example, "us" is an object pronoun replacing the subject of the sentence. The correct sentence would be:*

We had a great time at the bowling alley.

NOTES:

(10) She spoke to the children very nice.

Adjective versus Adverb *mistakes are made when an adverb is used to describe a noun or when an adjective is used to modify a verb, adjective, or another verb. In our example, nice is used incorrectly as an adjective; adjectives are used to describe (pro)nouns, but we're describing the verb, spoke. Thus, the corrected sentence would read:*

She spoke to the children very nicely.

Likewise, if we had an example such as:

The woman was very kindly.

we would have to recognize that "kindly" is describing "The woman," a noun, and thus an adjective must be used:

The woman was very kind.

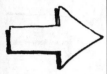

(11) All of the cats has a personal food dish.

Subject-Verb Agreement *refers to the subject and the verb in a sentence having the same plurality. This sample sentence errs as "cats has" is a plurality disagreement. The sentence can be corrected in two ways:*

All of the cats *have* a personal food dish.

or

Each of the cats *has* a personal food dish.

As a refresher, pronouns and nouns, as well as verbs and subjects, must indicate the same value (i.e. singular or plural).

NOTES:

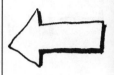

(12) If we all show fewer attention to our own happiness and more attention to the basic needs of others, less people will starve on the streets of the richest nation on the planet.

Less and Fewer *refer, respectively, to that which is uncountable and that which is quantifiable. This example misuses both forms. The amount of attention we show any one thing cannot be quantified whereas people can be enumerated. Therefore, the correct sentence would be:*

> If we all show less attention to our own happiness and more attention to the basic needs of others, fewer people will starve on the streets of the richest nation on the planet.

NOTES:

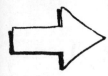

(13) Part-time jobs help students in their early teens develop fiscal constraint by learning the true value of money, social responsibility by adhering to a strict schedule and being obedient to management, and learning to take pride from a hard day of work.

Noun Parallelism is the same concept as verb parallelism, but applied to lists of nouns instead of verbs. In our example, we have a list that simplifies to:

> Fiscal constraint, social responsibility, and *learning to* take pride.

Hopefully the issue is now more clear. Our nouns (yep, nouns because they are the ideas or concepts of constraint/responsibility) fall out of parallel order when "learning to" comes into play. The correct sentence would be:

> Part-time jobs help students in their early teens develop fiscal constraint by learning the true value of money, social responsibility by adhering to a strict schedule and being obedient to management, and a sense of pride from a hard day of work.

To help discover errors in lists, attempt to quickly simplify the objects as done above. The extra details can easily distract from the grammatical error.

NOTES:

(14) They're car is entirely too small to fit all of the band equipment.

There, They're, and Their *are some of the most confusing words for ACT takers. There* is an adverb which refers to a location; this can be remembered by recognizing that the location "here" is one letter away from "there." *They're* is a contraction which breaks apart to mean "they are;" to differentiate, recognize the use of an apostrophe, indicating the presence of two words. *Their* is a possessive pronoun which describes a noun; note that *their* is the only one with an i, I being a pronoun. Therefore, the corrected sentence is:

> Their car is entirely too small to fit all of the band equipment.

Since "their car" could be replaced with a more-specific "John's car," we know the correct there/they're/their must be the one which replaced the pronoun, i.e. "their."

NOTES:

(15) I have two siblings—Jack and Steven—but he is taller.

Unclear Pronoun Reference occurs when one of two or more pronouns is replaced with an ambigious noun without a reference. In this sentence, "he" could refer to either Jack or Steven. To indicate which we are referring to, we must maintain the pronoun and say:

I have two siblings—Jack and Steven—but Jack is taller.

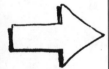

(16) The viewers were deeply effected by the whaling video footage.

Affect and Effect mean "to influence" and "a result," respectively. Just remember that an affect comes before an effect (chronologically speaking), the same way in which A comes before E in the alphabet. And since our sentence is referring to a video influencing the people, our correct sentence is:

The viewers were deeply affected by the whaling video footage (the effect of which was a series of protests).

Furthermore (though this does complicate things a bit), effect can also be used in rare instances to mean "to accomplish," as in, "Her goal was to effect a decrease in artificial fertilizers on the farm." However, this is less likely to be seen on the ACT, so don't hyperventilate.

(17) It is of utmost importance that you adhere with the rules!

Prepositional Idioms *are impossible to know without prior exposure; they are developed based solely on traditional usage and thus follow no definable rules. This example mistakes the prepositional idiom "adhere to" for "adhere with." The correct statement is:*

It is of utmost importance that you adhere to the rules!

NOTES:

To learn the common prepositional idioms, take time to periodically study the following list.

according to
accountable for [action]
accountable to [person]
adapt to [situation]
adhere to
adverse to
afraid of
anxious about
apologize for [thing]
apologize to [person]
approve of
aware of
be dependent on
blame [person] for [thing]
bored with
capable of
compete with
complain about
composed of
compete with
complain about
composed of
concentrate on
concerned with
congratulate on
conscious of
correspond to [thing]

correspond with [person]
consist of
deal with
depend (up)on
engaged to [person]
engaged in [activity]
equal to
fond of
from now on
frown (up)on
full of
glance at [thing]
glance through [thing]
grateful for [thing]
grateful to [person]
in accordance with
in conflict
in the habit of
in the near future
incapable of
inconsistent with
independent of
inferior to
insistent (up)on
interested in
knowledge of
next to

occupied by [thing]
occupied with [action] on
opposite of
part with [thing]
prior to
proceed to [action]
proceed with [thing]
prohibit from
proud of
regard to
related to
rely (up)on
respect for
responsible for
satisfied with
similar to
sorry for
surrounded by [people]
surrounded with [things]
suspicious of
take care of
tired of
top of
wait at [place]
wait for [thing]
with regard to

After training yourself to pay attention to these rules, begin exercising your mind's ear. Read the words of your favorite novelists and appreciate their adherence to the rules; read some of your old homework assignments, recognize the errors, and correct them. The English section is entirely reliant on your ability to recognize when writing goes awry; thus, this statement is going to get old, but it's good as gold: *practice makes perfect*. Go read!

ADDITIONAL ENGLISH TIPS

There are a few simple rules and tips that will carry you a long way in completing the English section of the ACT.

- <u>SCAN</u>. Prior to carefully reading a piece of prose and picking out details, take a few seconds (literally seconds; it shouldn't be a detailed reading whatsoever) and skim the whole passage. Once you have an idea of the piece's purpose, return to the beginning and read more carefully. This will help put the information into context from the very first sentence and cut down on time spent re-reading sentences out of confusion. It may also be helpful to glance at the questions prior to re-reading so you know what information to give more attention.

NOTES:

- <u>INSTINCTS</u>. As you read more thoroughly, let your instincts take over. Some sentences will be askew in one sense or another and any keen instinct will catch the ACT writers' tricks.

  - Is there something strange about the wording? Is there something about the sentence that makes you wonder if a robot or an alien is speaking to you? The proper use of language shouldn't cause you to cringe! (Note: The ACT is based on "standard English," so certain regional dialect peculiarities must be watched closely. If your everyday language differs from the idioms listed on page 98, put forth extra effort in relearning the standard English version.)

  - Are the ideas expressed in logical sequence—including chronological sequence, where applicable? Do the thoughts flow, or do you feel like you're reading the ramblings of an insane scientist? The prose isn't designed to mimic Thoreau's work; it's chosen for simplicity. Logical writing will have all of its aspects in a harmonious tone, tense, formality, and plurality.

NOTES:

- <u>BREVITY</u>. Be on the look-out for concise writing. We all used to add fluff to our papers to reach that page minimum; in the real world, however, wordiness is the *worst*. Almost a third of the ACT English section tests your ability to recognize fluff when you see it—so run far, far away from the longest answer provided (it's probably a trick). Concise writing avoids the following:

  - Superfluous information – Don't mention irrelevant ideas.

  - Content repetition – Don't say it more than once.

  - Verbosity – Don't get wordy and waste your wind.

  These rules are particularly important when dealing with English questions in the *<u>underlined</u>* passage format. The first question you should ask yourself prior to seeking grammatical correctness is, "Does this material stick out like a third wheel on an awkward date?" Yes? No? Well, when in doubt, take it out.

NOTES:

- <u>SENSE</u>. Whenever an *underlined* passage seems relevant to the completeness of an idea, it's time to ask, "Does this make any sense?" Often, the ACT writers will present information in a manner that can be easily comprehended without actually making one bit of sense. For example:

Each patron stopped to pet the dog as he or she walked into the coffee shop. Though his breath smelled *terrible. Even the* President could not resist his velvet ears.

A quick skim of this passage would likely provide you with enough information to make sense of the content; however, "Though his breath smelled terrible" is not a complete sentence, nor is it superfluous as it provides extra, relevant detail. Thus, we would bypass "OMIT" and choose "terrible, even the" as the correction.

- <u>TONE</u>. As you read a passage, be sensitive to its tone. Some questions will test your ability to recognize when (in)formal language is inappropriate. For example, never choose "NO CHANGE" if you're reading an excerpt from an encyclopedia and you see

> Shakespeare's *Hamlet* changed the world's view of power. Even his toughest critics declared this moving prose to be <u>bomb-diggity</u>.

Clearly the underlined slang is entirely inappropriate for the tone of the passage and should thus be changed.

- <u>EXPECTATIONS</u>. Sometimes you will be asked whether or not a certain sentence (usually the last) of a paragraph is appropriate considering the purpose and tone of the passage. For these questions, your skim-and-reread will be very helpful. Simply ask yourself, "Would I expect this statement?" If it seems to be a total tangent or takes on the voice of a stranger, look for the answer which best fits your instinct.

- <u>PURPORT</u>. Every so often, a Reading question will be embedded in the English section of the ACT. These questions will inquire about the meaning of the passage as a whole rather than nitpicking the grammar. For example, a passage may be followed by:

> This prose is best defined as early American colonist literature because it:
>   A. speaks of the native people's struggle with the colonists due to disease and land disputes.
>   B. chronicles Great Britain's pursuit of resources in a foreign land.
>   C. documents the struggles of the colonists upon arrival in a harsh environment.
>   D. contrasts the beliefs of Puritans and Quakers.

Clearly you cannot answer this question without having read the passage semi-thoroughly to differentiate between contextual information and the actual purpose of the prose.

NOTES:

Congratulations, you've just made it through the first section of the ACT! It wasn't as bad as you thought it would be, now was it? Hang in there, feller: it's a bit of a journey to get through this test, but we promise it'll be well worth it some day. And when you finally realize the value of the knowledge you've gained from this text, feel free to send us a thank you letter. Perhaps with a little bonus? (We used to say "Cash only, please," but Double Delight cupcakes have become increasingly popular!)

Check out your preparedness by completing another practice drill in the TPS workbook. Where did you stand when you completed section one? Where do you stand today? And what does this information tell you about your future planning?

CHAPTER 8

Math

TEST PREP
SEMINARS®

Before we begin, can we agree to view math as
nothing more than a series of puzzles? Really—think
of mathematics as a brainteaser and it goes from
dreadful to delightful. OK, maybe that's a tidbit of an
exaggeration—but it does help! So, got it? Good. Now
let's read these directions and have some nerdy fun!

So you know the directions...

Directions: *Solve each of the following problems, select the correct answer, and then fill in the corresponding space on your answer sheet.*

Note: Unless otherwise noted, all of the following should be assumed:

    1. Illustrative figures are not necessarily drawn to scale.

    2. All geometric figures lie in a plane.

    3. The term line indicates a straight line.

    4. The term average indicates arithmetic mean.

memorize the **DIRECTIONS**

Pretty straight forward, huh? You get 60 minutes to do 60 problems. The 60 questions cover material that is typically included in high school lesson plans prior to senior year (meaning no fancy calculus and very little trigonometry). To encompass 3+ years of material, the range of concepts for the math section is quite vast— but it's equally shallow.

The questions are divvied up like this:

> 24 – Pre-Algebra/Elementary Algebra
> 18 – Intermediate Algebra/Coordinate Geometry
> 18 – Plane Geometry/Trigonometry*
>
> *Trigonometry only has 4 questions. How nice is *that*?

Each of the sections listed above receives a sub-score. From the three sub-scores, an overall test score—your composite Math score—is reported.

Speaking of scores, remember that time the clock ran out and your algebra teacher had to rip your half-finished exam from your terrified hands? How did *THAT* feel? And then you got it back two days later, defaced with a giant, red F? (Hopefully not.) Well, the math section of the ACT isn't going to be like that. As a matter of fact, with 60 questions packed into 60 minutes, the math section goes unfinished by approximately 75% of students (a phenomena which can be attributed to students spending far too much time on difficult questions). Consequently, answering only about 55% of the questions correctly will earn you the national average score. Hence, you need not worry when you're finishing problem 42 and the two-minute warning is called. Just randomly fill those remaining bubbles; a random guess is better than no guess.

NOTES:

Unlike other subjects, the math questions tend to increase in difficulty (this is not to say, however, that there won't be those jarring road bumps in the midst of easy questions). Even though Pre-Algebra is inarguably easier than Trigonometry, the section isn't necessarily grouped according to topic. Different levels of questions—fundamentals, application, and analysis— spread the six topics from start to finish.

Test Prep Alert: This means you should avoid spending a full 60 seconds on any question from the first few pages. Don't linger over problems that are too time-consuming. (Move along, folks, nothing to see here.) Instead, fly through the easy ones first and throw your extra time into a reserve to be tapped later when you have time to go back to questions that require more time or analysis.

NOTES:

We're sure you've noticed by now that this math section is proportionally larger than the others. This is for a good reason: with dedication, students can generally raise their ACT math score more than any other section's score. And with that, you should feel inspired to read what's to come. Onward!

NOTES:

MATHEMATICALLY SPEAKING

Some questions will be relatively easy as they rely solely on the strength of your vocabulary. So take a minute to review these quick, calculation-free questions and get fluent in the language of mathematicians.

Prime Numbers – Positive numbers that can be evenly divided only by themselves _and_ one (note: themselves _and_ one, thus 1 is disqualified because, well, 1 and 1 are one in the same).
> » Prime: 7. Only divisible by 7 and 1.
> » Not Prime: 8. Divisible by 1, 2, 4, and 8.

Whole Numbers – Also known as natural/counting numbers.
> » 0, 1, 2, 3, 4 …

Integers – Whole numbers from negative infinity to positive infinity.
> » -∞ … -3, -2, -1, 0, 1, 2, 3, … ∞
> » -1½ and 85.3 are not integers because they are fractions/decimals.

Rational Numbers – All numbers that can be expressed as a fraction, terminating decimal, or a repeating decimal.
> » 1 ÷ 3 is rational because 0.3333... is an infinitely repeating decimal.

Irrational Numbers – Numbers that cannot be expressed with a fraction, terminating decimal, or a repeating decimal.

> » π = 3.14159265358979323384626433832...
> Clearly there is no repetition in the decimals;
> thus, π (pi) is irrational.

Remainders – The left-overs of a division process that does not end cleanly at the decimal place. Remainders are reported as an integer, not as a decimal.

> »
> $$\begin{array}{r} 6 \\ 4\overline{)27} \\ -24 \\ \hline 3 \end{array}$$
> Since any further division would require a decimal, the remainder is the left over 3.

Square Root ($\sqrt{\ }$) – A term which, when multiplied by itself, produces the radicand (term under root symbol). A square root has two answers—the positive root and the negative root—but refers only to the positive square root (unless otherwise indicated).

> » $\sqrt{49} = 7$ ($7 \times 7 = 49$)
> » $\sqrt{36} = 6$ ($6 \times 6 = 36$)

Word Problems – These "stories," which account for a third of the section, will describe a scenario which you must translate into a mathematical expression. Try to ignore the logical content of the stories—you'll just make yourself crazy. These problems require you to identify "knowns" and "unknowns." You must also be able to assign these (un)knowns variables to represent their relationship with one another. The phrases found below will help you with this process.

- *Increase, sum, exceeds, more than,* and *is greater than by* mean **addition**.

   Example: There are four more pens on her desk than there are pencils.

   We definitely don't know anything about pencils. So pencils can be our unknown, *x*. We do, however, know something about pens in relation to pencils: there are four more pens than pencils. Therefore, our known can be pens, which we'll call *y*.

   $$x = \text{pencils} \quad x + 4 = y = \text{pens}$$

- *Less than* means **subtraction**.

   Example: There are four less bottles than there were yesterday. We now have 3.

   All that we know is the current number of bottles, T. To get to the number *prior* to four of them were used, we can set up an equation in which the original number of bottles (which we will assign Y) is manipulated by removing four. We can then set this equal to the final number of bottles.

   T = bottles, today = 3
   Y = bottles, yesterday = T + 4 = 3 + 4 = 7

• *Times, product,* and *of* mean **multiplication**.

> **Example:** The product of two whole numbers is also equal to four more than six.
>
> In this example, we know that "product" indicates that two numbers are going to be multiplied and "more than" means they are being added.
>
> X × Y = 4 + 6

- Per means **fraction** (aka **division**).

    Example: If you're having a hard time paying attention, consider this: seven tiny, evil robots will invade your bedrooom per day until you shape-up and get to studying. How many days can you slack until your delinquent ways put you in a pickle? (For our purposes, 1 metric pickle is equal to 35 robots, which just so happens to be the number that fit under your bed and out of your parents' sight.)

    We can label the number of days L (for lazy-you-be, you see).

    Knowing that "per" is a ratio (which can be represented as a fraction), we have

$$\frac{(7 \text{ robots})}{\text{day}} \times L = 35 \text{ robots}$$

$$\frac{(35 \text{ robots})}{(7 \text{ robots/day})} = L$$

$$\frac{(35 \text{ \sout{robots}})}{1} \times \frac{(1 \text{ day})}{(7 \text{ \sout{robots}})} = L$$

$$L = 5 \text{ days}$$

That's right—you only get 5 days until there are so many tiny, evil robots crammed under your bed that they begin spilling out onto the floor and signal to your parents that you're *so* not allowed to go out on the weekends until you finish college.

This vocabulary, unlike that in English, is actually important to know by *name* because the ACT frequently asks questions such as, "which of the following numbers is a prime number?" or "which of these values is an irrational number?" It's *probably* important to know this material if it's the foundation of the subject most widely covered in the math section of the ACT (just saying). Before reading on, try making flash cards or composing a little ditty; after all, these vocabulary questions will be the quickest and easiest points to nab.

NOTES:

PEMDAS

PRE-ALGEBRA

Stuff you may have forgotten, but will need to know!

Let's take a walk down memory lane...

1.) PLEASE EXCUSE MY DEAR AUNT SALLY

This mnemonic device specifies the order of operations:

Parenthesis **E**xponents **M**ultiplication **D**ivision **A**ddition **S**ubtraction

Always, *always,* *always* adhere to the order of operations. Not performing your arithmetic in the correct sequence will most definitely give you an answer which you'll find to be one of the multiple choice options—but unfortunately, it'll be the wrong one.

This warning extends to calculator use, as well. For example, plugging the equation

$$3 + 7^2 \times 4 - 3 \times 2$$

into many calculators will give you an answer of 410. However, correctly following the order of operations will will give you a much different answer of 193—so beware!

If you run into a situation in which multiples of any one given operation exist, simply perform the computations as you read them from left to right. If parenthetical data is *within* parenthetical data, begin at the core of the problem and work your way out of the parenthesis/brackets. The order of operations is valid for each layer of parenthesis.

 (Note: The division bar can be treated like a parenthesis; if there are operations under a division bar, consider it parenthesized.

Furthermore, the root function is considered an exponent, as $\sqrt{3}$ can be rewritten as $3^{½}$, so calculate roots during the same step as exponents).

Example: $2 \times 3^3 + (7 + [3 \times 2 + 1])^2 - 2(3^2 + 10) \div \sqrt{36}$

P: There are two sets of parenthesis, one with an inner set. Begin clearing them, starting with the core set of parenthesis:

$$[3 \times 2 + 1] = 6 + 1 = 7$$
$$2 \times 3^3 + (7 + 7)^2 - 2(3^2 + 10) \div \sqrt{36}$$
$$2 \times 3^3 + 14^2 - 2(9 + 10) \div \sqrt{36}$$
$$2 \times 3^3 + 14^2 - 2(19) \div \sqrt{36}$$

E: There are three exponents here; clearing them:

$$2 \times 27 + 14^2 - 2(19) \div \sqrt{36}$$
$$2 \times 27 + 196 - 2(19) \div 36^{\frac{1}{2}}$$
$$2 \times 27 + 196 - 2(19) \div 6$$

(Later we will discuss roots as exponents; hang in there.)

M/D: Performing all multiplication and division from left to right:

$$54 + 196 - 38 \div 6$$
$$54 + 196 - \frac{38}{6}$$

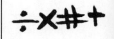

A/S: Performing all addition and subtraction:

$$250 - \frac{38}{6} = \frac{250}{1}\left(\frac{6}{6}\right) - \frac{38}{6}$$

$$\frac{1500}{6} - \frac{38}{6} = \frac{1462}{6} = 243\frac{2}{3}$$

2.) Factors & Multiples

A **factor** is a number which can divide evenly into another number.

4 is a factor of 20; 4 can be factored from 20 a total of five times. 20 ÷ 4 = 5

2 is a factor of 6; 2 can be factored from 6 a total of three times. 6 ÷ 2 = 3

A **multiple** is the product of two numbers.

12 is a multiple of 6. 6 × 2 = 12

99 is a multiple of 11. 11 × 9 = 99

3.) Fractions

Addition/Subtraction: To perform addition and subtraction on fractions, it is necessary to achieve a least common denominator (LCD, the smallest multiple which the fractions' denominators share). The operation may then be performed across the numerator and the LCD can simply be transferred into the new numerator.

$$\frac{1}{3} + \frac{4}{5} = \left(\frac{5}{5}\right)\left(\frac{1}{3}\right) + \left(\frac{3}{3}\right)\left(\frac{4}{5}\right) = \frac{5}{15} + \frac{12}{15} = \frac{17}{15}$$

Multiplication: Multiply the numerators (numbers on the top of the fraction) and this is your product's numerator; multiply the denominators (numbers on the bottom of the fraction) and this is your product's denominator. The answer in your booklet will be in the simplest form; so, always simplify your work.

$$\frac{3}{4} \times \frac{4}{5} = \frac{12}{20} = \frac{3}{5}$$

Division: Take the reciprocal of the second fraction (e.g., swap the numerator and denominator) and continue as if solving a multiplication problem.

$$\frac{6}{7} \div \frac{2}{9} = \frac{6}{7} \times \frac{9}{2} = \frac{54}{14} = \frac{27}{7}$$

4.) Cross-Multiplication

Cross-multiplication is used when two fractions, one or both containing a variable, are set equal to each other. This method achieves equal denominators. By having the numerators in equal terms, the denominator can be ignored and basic Algebra can be used to solve for the variable(s). Simply multiply both sides by the opposite's denominator and forget that you ever had any denominators at all.

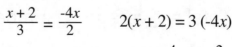

$$\frac{x+2}{3} = \frac{-4x}{2} \qquad 2(x + 2) = 3 \, (-4x)$$

$$2x + 4 = -12x \qquad x = -\frac{4}{14} = -\frac{2}{7}$$

NOTES:

5.) Arithmetic Sequences

If a sequence of numbers has a constant difference in consecutive terms, it is an arithmetic sequence. The formula you will need to use is

$$a_n = a_1 + (n - 1)d$$

a_n = value in the sequence
a_1 = first term the sequence
n = n^{th} term you are seeking
d = common difference

With enough information about a sequence, this equation can be used to find the sequence's n^{th} term—even if n^{th} is equal to million. See the example below.

Given the following sequence, find the 82nd term.
12, 18, 24, 30, 36 ...

Our difference, d, is found by recognizing that each consecutive term increases by 6.

$$a_n = 12 + (82 - 1)6 = 12 + (81)6 = 12 + 486 = 498$$

6.) Mean, Median, Mode, & Range

Mean is just a fancy way of saying *average*. To calculate the mean, add all values together and divide by the number of values involved. To remember this concept, just think:

memorize

TAN = <u>T</u>otal = <u>A</u>verage × <u>N</u>umber of Items

With a bit of arithmetic, this equation can be manipulated to give you either the average or the number of items.

Median is the middle number. Place all values in order of least to greatest and cross them off from either end until you meet in the middle. If there is an even number of values, the median is found by taking the two "medians" and averaging them.

Mode is the number which recurs most frequently. If no number appears more than once, there is no mode.

Range is the magnitude of a set of values; it is found by subtracting the lowest value from the highest.

Example: Find the mean, median, mode, and range of the following values: 2, 12, 4, 7, 2, & 9.

Mean: $(2 + 12 + 4 + 7 + 2 + 9) \div 6 = 6$

Median: ~~2~~ 2 4 7 ~~9~~ ~~12~~ $(4 + 7) \div 2 = 5.5$

Mode: 2 appears most often.

Range: $12 - 2 = 10$

7.) Absolute Value

Absolute Value, identified via vertical bars (|x|), represents the distance of a value from zero when plotted on a number line. Since there is no such thing as a negative distance, all absolute values will be positive.

$$|-12| = 12 \qquad |12| = 12 \qquad |0| = 0 \qquad |-x| = x$$

NOTES:

Absolutely

NOTES:

8.) Percentages

You will frequently be asked to increase or decrease a value by some percentage. If you're feeling iffy about this, consider how often you use this skill in the real world. Shopping, anyone? (No, that's not a cue for you to go buy a new pair of kicks—sit back down!) If something is on sale, you have to first subtract the sale percent-off from the original price; from that value, you then calculate and tack on the tax.

> What is the price of a $39 jacket after being reduced 40%? Include a sales tax of 5.1%.

$39 - 39(.40) =$ To find the percentage of x in a group
$39 - 15.60 = 23.40$ of y, use the following: $x \div y \times 100\%$.
$23.40 + 23.40(.051) =$ Remember that percentages are
$23.40 + 1.19 = \$24.59$ parts of 100, i.e. $5.1/100 = 5.1\%$.

If you are dealing with a problem that simply states "a percentage" without ever telling you the whole value, assume it is 100 and manipulate the 100 stepwise.

> If 40% of the books are sold, but 20% of those sold were returned, what percentage represents the coffee shop's net sale?

> $100(.40) = 40\%$ sold
> $40(.20) = 8\%$ returned
> $40 - 8 = 32\%$ of the books were successfully sold.

9.) Averages

You're unlikely to receive a question as easy as, "what is the average of 1, 2, and 3?" What you're more likely to see is an average value and all but one of its components. In this case, you'll have to find the missing value.

The five waitresses pool their tips at The Marina and split the earnings evenly. Tonight, they each made $67 on average, during the Saturday rush. If two waitresses made $73 each, one made $64, and one made $69, how much did the fifth waitress add to the tip pool?

    A. $51
    B. $53
    C. $56
    D. $69
    E. $72

If they are splitting the tips evenly, they are each taking an average amount. To determine the fifth waitress' input, we must determine which amount (which we'll assign the variable Z) is necessary to make the average of the tips be $67.

$$67 = ([73 \times 2] + 64 + 69 + Z) \div 5$$
$$67 \times 5 = 146 + 64 + 69 + Z$$
$$335 = 279 + Z$$
$$56 = Z$$

And our fifth waitress makes out well, putting $56 into the tip jar and leaving with $67—answer C.

10.) Weighted Averages

Beware of weighted averages as they cannot be treated the same way that we deal with basic averages. Weighted average problems typically ask for a combined average of pre-averaged values, and it is almost always incorrect to average the averages as is. Rather, you need to backtrack to the original values and work from there.

A pet store has three litters of kittens: one with 6, one with 4, and one with 3. The store feeds the first litter an average of 7.4 ounces of wet food per kitten per day, the second litter 8.2 ounces, and the third litter 10.1 ounces. What does the pet store feed each of its kittens on average?

F. 8.2 ounces

G. 8.3 ounces

H. 8.6 ounces

J. 8.7 ounces

K. 8.8 ounces

Simply averaging the three given values would not account for the smallest amount being eaten by twice as many kittens as the largest amount. To do so, we must undo the average of each litter and *then* find the average.

$$(6[7.4] + 4[8.2] + 3[10.1]) \div (6 + 4 + 3) =$$
$$(44.4 + 32.8 + 30.3) \div (13) =$$

$$107.5 \div 13 = 8.3 \text{ ounces per cat.}$$

Thus our answer is G (*not* F, because 8.269 rounds up to 8.3). If we had foregone taking the weight of the averages into account, we would end up with…

$$(7.4 + 8.2 + 10.1) \div 3 = 25.7 \div 3 = 8.6$$

…which, unsurprisingly, is one of the options—and will be on the actual exam. Don't fall for it!

11.) Probabilities

Do not be intimidated by probability problems. Just keep two things in mind:

1. Probabilities are represented as part-over-whole ratios, and
2. Past events do not affect future probabilities, unless the event has altered the scenario permanently.

Let's try the following to clarify these two rules:

If there are 5 delicious cherry suckers in a bag of 35 other not-so-delicious suckers, what is the probability that I will find deliciousness when I reach into the bag?

Part: 5 cherry suckers

Whole: 40 suckers (5 cherry and 35 not-so-delicious flavored)

Probability: 5/40 (or, simplified, 1/8)

NOTES:

I reach into the bag and pull out a root beer sucker. I shove my hand back into the bag, release the not-so-delicious sucker, and return to my search for a cherry sucker. What is the probability that I will find one?

> Past events do not affect probabilities if nothing has changed in the scenario. If the parts and the whole never change, the probability is the same—even if we just happen to reach into the bag 50 times and never find a cherry sucker. Therefore, we're still reaching in at a 1/8 probability that we'll find deliciousness.

When I pull out my hand, I see a grape sucker. Since they're my best friend's favorite, I give it to her. One sucker missing from the bag, I dive back in. What is the probability of me finding deliciousness?

> The whole has changed this time, from 40 to 39, so our probability becomes 5/39.

12.) Ratios

Used to compare two numbers, ratios can be written in three different forms: "X:Y," "X/Y," and "X to Y." The only thing you need to keep in mind for ratios is that they can be manipulated via multiplication and division as long as whatever is done to X is also done to Y (e.g. The ratio 1:2 can be multiplied on either side by 2 to obtain 2:4).

13.) Exponents, Logarithms, & Roots

Exponents can be read as, "multiply this number by itself *n* number of times."

$$3^4 = 3 \times 3 \times 3 \times 3 = 81 \qquad 4^2 = 4 \times 4 = 16$$

Keep in mind these three rules:

1. Any number to the zero power is always equal to 1.
$$35325^0 = 1 \qquad 1^0 = 1$$

2. Any number to the first power is equal to itself.
$$5^1 = 5 \qquad 537587^1 = 537587$$

3. A negative exponent is made positive by moving the base value from the numerator to the denominator, or vice versa.

$$5^{-1} = \frac{1}{5}$$

$$\left(\frac{9}{4}\right)^{-\frac{1}{2}} = \left(\frac{4}{9}\right)^{\frac{1}{2}} = \frac{\sqrt{4}}{\sqrt{9}} = \frac{2}{3}$$

Logarithms are another way to express exponents. They aren't frequently tested on the ACT, but they're quite easy to convert to and from exponents; so, you might as well be prepared. Use the following conversion:

$$\log_x Y = Z \quad \leftrightarrow \quad X^Z = Y$$

Roots are also exponents, but they are fractions with a numerator of 1 and denominator of any value. Denoted with a radical $(\sqrt{x})$, the root value is altered based on the number written above the radical's tail $(\sqrt{})$. If no number is specified, the root is an understood square/2nd root. Roots represent a number which must be multiplied by itself n times $(\sqrt[n]{})$ to achieve some given value, e.g., $\sqrt[3]{8} = 2$ because 2 x 2 x 2 = 8. There are two rules to remember:

1. Even roots have both a positive and a negative answer; however, unless otherwise stated, only the positive root is being referenced/sought on the ACT.

2. A negative number under an even radical is an imaginary number and cannot be represented without the use of *i*. If the radical is odd, however, the root will just be negative. (If *i* is new to you, don't be too upset; the ACT *rarely* tests students on this concept. We just included imaginary numbers for the sake of this graphic....and just in case.)

$$\sqrt{-36} \ = \ \sqrt{-1} \ \times \ \sqrt{36} \ = \ 6i$$

$$\sqrt[3]{-8} \ = \ -2$$

NOTES:

14.) Linear Equations

A linear equation is an expression with one or more variables raised to the first power. To solve a linear equation, observe the following steps:

1. Move all terms with the analyzed variable to one side of the equal sign.

2. Move all other variables and/or constants to the other side.

3. If the coefficient on the analyzed variable is not 1, divide both sides by the coefficient to achieve an isolated analyzed variable.

$$Solve\ for\ y. \quad 3x + 2 = 4y + 4$$
$$3x - 2 = 4y$$
$$\tfrac{3}{4}x - \tfrac{1}{2} = y$$

ELEMENTARY ALGEBRA

1.) Manipulating Exponents

Addition/Subtraction: If and only if the variable and exponent are the same
(i.e., $13x^3$ and $8x^3$ versus $13y^3$ and $8x^3$ or $13x^4$ and $8x^3$),
addition and subtraction of exponential terms may be performed like so:

- Addition: Add the coefficients of like terms, leaving the variable and exponent intact.
$$2x^2 + 4x^3 + 6x^2 = (2 + 6)x^2 + 4x^3 = 8x^2 + 4x^3$$

- Subtraction: Subtract the coefficients of like terms, leaving the variable and exponent intact.
$$13x^6 - 1x^4 - 8x^4 = 13x^6 + (-1 - 8)x^4 = 13x^6 - 9x^4$$

Multiplication/Division: If and only if the variables are the same (i.e., $2x^4 \times 5x^4$ versus $2y^4 \times 5x^4$), multiplication and division can be performed in the following manner:

- Multiplication: Multiply the coefficients and add the exponents. $(ax^n)(bx^m) = (a \times b)x^{(n+m)}$
$$4z^1 \times 2z^2 = (4 \times 2)z^{(1 + 2)} = 8z^3$$

- Division: Divide the coefficients and subtract the exponents. $ax^n \div bx^m = (a \div b)x^{(n-m)}$
$$10w^{12} \div 2w^4 = (10 \div 2)w^{(12 - 4)} = 5w^8$$

NOTES:

Power to a Power: Put any coefficients to the super exponent and multiply the exponent by the super exponent. $(ax^n)^m = (a^n x^{(n \times m)})$

$$(3x^6)^2 = 3^2 x^{(6 \times 2)} = 9x^{12}$$

With this knowledge, you should be able to simplify an equation such as

$$[14x^2 + (2x^3)^3] \div 2x^2 - 13x^5 \times 4x^9 + x^5$$
$$= [14x^2 + 2^3 x^{3 \times 3}] \div 2x^2 - 13 \times 4x^{5+9} + x^5$$
$$= [14x^2 + 8x^9] \div 2x^2 - 52x^{14} + x^5$$
$$= [(14 \div 2)x^{2-2} + (8 \div 2)\, x^{9-2}] - 52x^{14} + x^5$$
$$= 7x^0 + 4x^7 - 52x^{14} + x^5$$
$$= 7 + 4x^7 - 52x^{14} + x^5$$

(Remember: Anything to the zero power is equal to 1.)

which, ordered by exponent value, is:

$$= -52x^{14} + 4x^7 + x^5 + 7$$

2.) Polynomials

Polynomials are expressions composed of constants and multiple variables and/or one variable with multiple positive, whole number exponents. You will need to manipulate these equations by simplification and distribution.

Simplification is the condensing of information by combining like terms, i.e., constants and all like variables with like exponents.

$$3x^3 + 2x - 13 - 4x + 5x^3$$
$$(3 + 5)x^3 + (2 - 4)x - 13$$
$$8x^3 - 2x - 13$$

Distribution is the multiplication of a factor outside of parenthesis with all items within the parenthesis.

$$4x(2x + 4y - 1)$$
$$(4x \times 2x) + (4x \times 4y) - (4x \times 1)$$
$$8x^2 + 16xy - 4x$$

3.) Multiplying Binomials

Multiplying binomials is only a matter of distribution. Use the FOIL method to ensure that you don't forget or double-up multiplication of any two given terms.

FOIL: First, Outer, Inner, Last

$$(x + 2)(x - 9) = ?$$

First: $(x + 2)(x - 9) = x^2$

Outer: $(x + 2)(x - 9) = x^2$ **- 9x**

Inner: $(x + 2)(x - 9) = x^2$ - 9x **+ 2x**

Last: $(x + 2)(x - 9) = x^2$ - 9x + 2x **- 18**

Simplify: $x^2 - 7x - 18$

NOTES:

4.) Evaluating Algebraic Expressions

You are either going to see, "if x = n, find y" or "evaluate f(n)." Both mean the same thing and should be treated accordingly: wherever you see x, replace it (in parenthesis, for distribution purposes) with n. Simplify.

$$f(x) = x^2 + 2x - 8. \text{ Evaluate } f(z + 3)$$
$$f(z + 3) = x^2 + 2x - 8$$
$$= (z + 3)^2 + 2(z + 3) - 8$$
$$= z^2 + 6z + 9 + 2z + 6 - 8$$
$$= z^2 + 8z + 7$$

Note: "f(x) =" is read as "function of x" and was some guy's big idea to make math a little more confusing. All it's really saying is "when the value inside of the parenthesis is substituted for all x's, y is equal to.."

For example, if f(x) = x + 1

and we are told to evaluate f(2),

we'd plug and chug: f(2) = (2) + 1 = 3.

plug and chug

5.) Factoring/Solving Quadratic Equations

There are three methods to solving quadratic equations: guessing, the AC test, and the Quadratic Formula. The first two are used for rational x values and the latter is for irrational x values as well as difficult to guess fractions. In all three cases, the first step is to set your equation equal to zero and rewrite it in the form of $Ax^2 + Bx + C$:

$$3x^2 + 3x - 5 = 2x - 3 \quad \rightarrow \quad 3x^2 + x - 2 = 0$$

For this example, A = 3, B = 1, and C = –2. Next, set up the framework for your factoring, which will be in the form of

$$(qx \pm s)(rx \pm t)$$

(*q* and *r* being coefficients and *s* and *t* being constants). For example, the above equation could be broken down to be

$$(3x - 2)(x + 1)$$

where q = 3, s= -2, r = 1, and t = 1.

From here, the methods are slightly different.

A) Guessing is the preferred method of factoring rational x values for number-savvy students. The name describes the step(s) in the method perfectly: you're literally going to guess values for *q, s, r,* and *t* (which we've represented as underlined slots), plug, and check.

$x^2 + 7x - 8 = 0$

$(\_x + \_\_)(\_x - \_\_) = 0$

$(x + 8)(x - 1) = 0$

$x + 8 = 0 \quad x - 1 = 0$

$x = \text{-}8 \quad \text{and} \quad x = 1$

Since *C* is negative, we know that *s* and *t* are of opposite signs. Additionally, since *B* is positive, we know that the larger of *s* and *t* must be positive.

and we check:

$(\text{-}8)^2 + 7(\text{-}8) - 8 = 0$

$64 - 56 - 8 = 0$

$64 - 64 = 0 \quad \text{good!}$

$(1)^2 + 7(1) - 8 = 0$

$1 + 7 - 8 = 0$

$8 - 8 = 0 \quad \text{good!}$

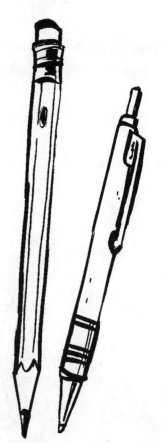

B) AC Test uses the following method to solve a quadratic equation (we'll use $2x^2 - 6x - 8$ as an example):

1. List all factors of A×C's product

     A×C = 2×8 = 16, factors of 16 = 1, 2, 4, 8, 16

2. Determine which two will add or subtract to give you the middle term, B.

     Using 2 and 8:

     B = –6 = 2 – 8

     Thus, 2 is positive and 8 is negative

3. Plug these values into the factor set and, if necessary, determine which set has a non-zero coefficient on x.

     (_x + 2)(_x – 4) = 0

     (2x + 2)(x – 4) = 0

     x = -1 and x = 4

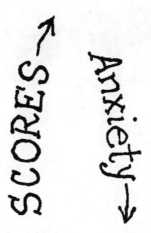

SCORES↗

Anxiety↓

NOTES:

C) **The Quadratic Equation** may be one of your most powerful tools on the ACT—especially if you've used it enough times to mentally perform half of the arithmetic prior to plugging values into the equation. Befriend this equation:

$$x = \frac{-B \pm \sqrt{B^2 - 4AC}}{2A}$$

(The ± sign, which means "plus or minus," gives you the two answers.)

And here is a sample problem which the quadratic equation solves quite nicely:

A rubber ball is thrown toward the ground from a height of 23.5 meters. If the ball's height at time *t* can be described with the equation

$$h(t) = -4.4t^2 + 14.9t + 34.8$$

how many seconds will pass until the ball hits the ground?

Since the ball will hit the ground at a height of zero, we can set $h=0$ and solve for t.

$$x = \frac{-14.9 \pm \sqrt{14.9^2 - 4(-4.4)(34.8)}}{2(-4.4)}$$

Plug in your A, B, & C values and solve.

$$x = \frac{-14.9 \pm \sqrt{222.01 + 612.48}}{-8.8}$$

$$x = \frac{-14.9 \pm \sqrt{834.49}}{-8.8}$$

$$x = \frac{-14.9 \pm 28.9}{-8.8}$$

$$x = -1.6 \quad or \quad x = 5.0$$

Lastly, since we cannot have a negative time, we can omit the -1.6 answer and report that the ball hits the ground after 5.0 seconds.

(Haha, we just tricked you into doing physics. How was it, smartypants?)

All three methods will get you to the same place, so use the one with which you feel most comfortable.

6.) Simplifying Algebraic Fractions

Always factor the numerator and denominator separately. Once both are fully factored, terms which appear in the numerator and denominator may be omitted as they cancel each other.

$$f(x) = \frac{x^2 - 4x - 32}{x^2 - 16} = \frac{(x+4)(x-8)}{(x+4)(x-4)} = \frac{(x-8)}{(x-4)}$$

7.) Solving Inequalities

An inequality shows the relationship between a variable and its context. This can be on a number line, on a graph, or even in reference to another variable. To solve an inequality, treat the inequality symbol as an equal sign and solve for the variable. The only trick to remember here is that <u>multiplying or dividing an inequality by a negative value switches the direction of the symbol</u>.

$-3x + 17 \leq 8$
$-3x \leq -9$ An <u>underlined</u> inequality denotes
$x \geq 3$ ($\leftarrow$ sign switch)   greater/less than <u>or equal to</u>.

To graph an inequality on a number line, arrange your inequality so that the x is on the left-hand side of the sign (if you swap the x and constant, remember to swap the sign's direction as well). The direction of the arrow will tell you which direction to shade on the number line. Furthermore, if the arrow is <u>underlined</u>, your circle on the constant will be closed; otherwise, it will be open.

3
$\longleftarrow$ ●$\longrightarrow$
$x \geq 3$ (correct)

3
$\longleftarrow$ ⊕$\longrightarrow$
$x \geq 3$ (incorrect)

Quadratic inequalities are solved by changing the inequality to an equal sign and factoring the quadratic equation. Once two factors are determined, place them on a number line to break our range of integers into three sections which we'll call *a, b,* and *c* (see below).

$$x^2 - 5x - 6 > 0$$

becomes

$$x^2 - 5x - 6 = 0$$
$$(x + 1)(x - 6) = 0$$
$$x = -1 \qquad x = 6$$

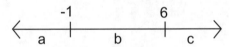

Check for truth in areas *a, b,* and *c* by taking a value within each and plugging it into the original equation.

area a: $f(-2) = 8 > 0$ True
area b: $f(0) = -6 > 0$ False
area c: $f(7) = 7 > 0$ True

And from these checks, we can say that our statement is true when

$$x < -1 \quad \text{or} \quad x > 6$$

Compound inequalities, which contain two or more inequality symbols, will also be covered in the ACT. These should be treated in the same manner as simple inequalities—just remember that you have multiple equal signs, and whatever you do to any section must be done to all other sections as well. After solving, graph both on the same line and shade *only where they **overlap***.

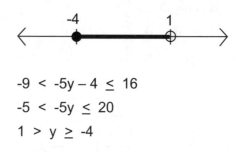

$$-9 < -5y - 4 \leq 16$$
$$-5 < -5y \leq 20$$
$$1 > y \geq -4$$

INTERMEDIATE ALGEBRA

1.) Differences of Squares & Perfect Square Binomials

To save yourself a plethora of time, memorize these equations:

$$A^2 - B^2 = (A + B)(A - B)$$

$$(A + B)^2 = A^2 + 2AB + B^2$$

$$(A - B)^2 = A^2 - 2AB + B^2$$

2.) Absolute Value Equations

Remember that taking the absolute value of a number simply negates any negative signs, thus reporting the distance of the value from the zero on a number line. If we are using the absolute value of some variable x, then we must take into account that either a negative or a positive value may be inside the absolute value brackets and solve accordingly. To do so, follow these steps:

1. Isolate the absolute value.

    $|x + 2| + 3 > 14$

    $|x + 2| > 11$

2. Rewrite the equation twice:

    (1) As is, without the absolute value brackets.

    $x + 2 > 11$

    (2) Prior to dropping the absolute value brackets, reverse the sign and multiply the right side of the equation by -1.

    $x + 2 < -11$

3. Solve for the variables. Rewrite as an "or" statement—as the value within the brackets is either positive or negative, not both.

    $x + 2 > 11$ or $x + 2 < -11$

    $x > 9$ $x < -13$

NOTES:

3.) System of Equations

A system of equations is the overlapping of two graphed equations or the use of one or more variables in two separate mathematical expressions. To solve a system of equations, we need to determine where a given value for each variable makes both mathematical expressions true statements. This can be done via two methods:

A) Elimination Method for the system

$$x - 25 = -3y \quad \& \quad x - 53 = -7y$$

1. Rewrite both equations in standard form $(Ax + By = C)$

$$x + 3y = 25 \quad \& \quad x + 7y = 53$$

2. Multiply one/both by factor(s) which will result in the coefficients on one of the variables becoming the positive and negative of a number.

(Note: The equations may be multiplied by different factors; just make sure to multiply the entire equation by the factor, not just the coefficient of interest.)

Seeking to eliminate the Y values, 3 and 7's least common multiple is 21; thus, multiply the equations by the factors which will achieve one +21y and one -21y.

$$7(x + 3y = 25) \quad \text{and} \quad -3(x + 7y = 53)$$

3. Vertically align these products and add downward.

$$7x + 21y = 175$$
$$\underline{+ \; -3x - 21y = -159}$$
$$4x \; + \; 0y \; = 16$$

or $4x = 16$

NOTES:

4. Solve for the remaining variable.

$$x = 4$$

5. Take the solved variable and plug it into one of the
original equations to solve for the other variable.

$$x + 3y = 25 (4) + 3y = 25 y = 7$$

6. To check your answer, take the resultants from steps 4
and 5 and plug them into the other original equation to
check for agreement.

$$x + 7y = 53 (4) + 7(7) = 53 53 = 53. \text{ Good!}$$

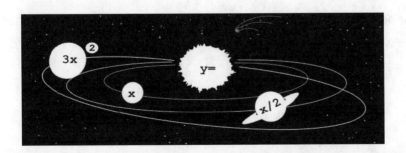

NOTES:

B) **Substitution Method** for the system

$$7y + x = 16 \quad \& \quad 2x - 10 = 8y$$

1. Solve for any variable in one of the equations.

   Choose wisely. The coefficient on x in the first equation is already one, so save some time and use it!

   $$x = 16 - 7y$$

2. Plug the identity of the solved variable from the first equation into the second equation wherever the variable exists.

   $$2(16 - 7y) - 10 = 8y$$

3. Solve for the remaining variable.

   $$32 - 14y - 10 = 8y$$
   $$22 = 22y$$
   $$y = 1$$

4. Take this variable and plug it into one of the original equations to solve for the remaining unknown.

   $$7y + x = 16 \qquad 7(1) + x = 16 \qquad x = 9$$

5. Be smart: perform a check.

   $$2x - 10 = 8y \quad 2(9) - 10 = 8(1) \quad 8 = 8 \text{ Good!}$$

Depending on the presentation of the problem, your answer may be written in the form (x, y) for a coordinate plane or in $x = n$ and $y = m$ for a word problem.

4.) Radical Expressions

Addition/Subtraction: When the radicand (value within the radical) and root are synonymous among multiple radical expressions, treat the radical as a variable and add/subtract accordingly. If the radicands or roots are dissimilar, they cannot be combined.

$$7\sqrt{3} + 2\sqrt{2} - 3\sqrt{3} + 6\sqrt{2} - 5\sqrt{7}$$
$$= 4\sqrt{3} + 8\sqrt{2} - 5\sqrt{7}$$

Multiplication/Division: When the root is synonymous, the coefficients and the radicands can be multiplied/divided normally (the coefficients and radicands treated separately).

$$3\sqrt[3]{2} \times 5\sqrt[3]{4}$$
$$= (3 \times 5)\ \sqrt[3]{(2 \times 4)}$$
$$= 15\sqrt[3]{8} \qquad = 15 \times 2 \qquad = 30$$

5.) Composite Functions

These operations simply insert one function into another.

If $f(x) = x^2 + 2x - 1$ and $g(x) = x + 2$, what is $f(g(x + 2))$?

$$g(x + 2) = (x + 2) + 2 = x + 4$$
$$f(x + 4) = (x + 4)^2 + 2(x + 4) - 1 = x^2 + 10x + 23$$

GOT THAT?

6.) Matrices

A matrix is a rectangular array of numbers used in linear algebra, geometric optics, etc. All you need to know (thankfully, right?) is how to perform basic arithmetic and distribution on them—and it's surprisingly easy, especially considering how intimidating matrices look.

For *addition/subtraction*, the position of the entries (also referred to as *elements*) are matched with those of the sister entry; those two entries are then combined via whichever operation is indicated.

$$\begin{bmatrix} x_{a1} & x_{a2} \\ x_{b1} & x_{b2} \end{bmatrix} + \begin{bmatrix} x_{c1} & x_{c2} \\ x_{d1} & x_{d2} \end{bmatrix} = \begin{bmatrix} x_{a1} + x_{c1} & x_{a2} + x_{c2} \\ x_{b1} + x_{d1} & x_{b2} + x_{d2} \end{bmatrix}$$

For *scalar multiplication,* in which a value is outside of a matrix, the matrix is operated upon via the distributive property.

$$k \begin{bmatrix} x_{a1} & x_{a2} \\ x_{b1} & x_{b2} \end{bmatrix} = \begin{bmatrix} kx_{a1} & kx_{a2} \\ kx_{b1} & kx_{b2} \end{bmatrix}$$

(Told you it's easy.)

COORDINATE GEOMETRY

1.) Slope

Represented by the letter m, slope is calculable for any two points, (x_1, y_1) and (x_2, y_2), on a Cartesian (or coordinate) plane via the equation:

$$m = \frac{\text{rise}}{\text{run}} = \frac{(y_2 - y_1)}{(x_2 - x_1)}$$

- A *positive slope* will rise in the direction of the **upper** right-hand corner.

- A *negative slope* falls toward the **bottom** right-hand corner.

- *Horizontal lines* have a slope of **zero** (0).

- *Vertical lines* have an **undefined** slope.

- *Parallel lines* share the **same** slope

- *Perpendicular lines* have **negative reciprocals** of each other's slope (e.g., if line$_1$ and line$_2$ are perpendicular, then $m_1 = A$ and $m_2 = {}^{-1}/_A$)

- If an equation is in **slope-intercept form** ($y = mx + b$), your slope is the **coefficient of x**.

NOTES:

2.) Distance Formula

The distance between two points can be found with the following equation:

$$d = \sqrt{(x_2 - x_1)^2 + (y_2 - y_1)^2}$$

For example, to find the distance between (-3, 4) & (6, 7):

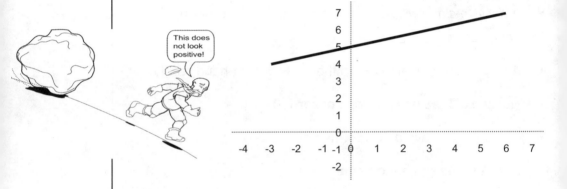

$$d = \sqrt{(6 - (-3))^2 + (7 - 4)^2}$$

$$= \sqrt{9^2 + 3^2}$$

$$= \sqrt{81 + 9}$$

$$= \sqrt{90}$$

$$= \sqrt{9} \times \sqrt{10}$$

$$= 3\sqrt{10}$$

Simplify radicals by rewriting them as a rational and an irrational term. The root is then taken on the first and placed in front of the second.

3.) Midpoint

To find the midpoint of a line between any two given points, average (separately) the x values and the y values.

$$\text{Midpoint} = \left(\frac{(x_1 + x_2)}{2} , \frac{(y_1 + y_2)}{2} \right)$$

4.) Circles and Curves

Unfortunately, you're going to have to memorize these two equations. Notice the similarities between them—it'll make the process easier.

Circle	$(x - h)^2 + (y - k)^2 = r^2$	(h,k) is the center; r is the radius.
Parabola	$y = a(x - h)^2 + k$ or $x = a(y - k)^2 + h$	(h,k) is the vertex for the first and (k,h) is the vertex for the second. The first equation is for parabolas which open upward (if a is positive) or downward (if a is negative); the second is for those which open right (if a is positive) and left (if a is negative).

formulas TO REMEMBER

PLANE GEOMETRY

Vocabulary:

Arc – A portion of a circle's circumference

Area – The space enclosed within a two-dimensional figure

Bisect – To divide into two equal parts

Circumference – The perimeter of, or distance around, a circle

Chord – A segment which begins and ends on two points along a circle's circumference and runs through the circle

Congruent – When superimposed, figures have identical shape and size

Diameter – The length of a line segment that passes through the center of a circle, beginning and ending on two points along the circumference

Equidistant – Equal in distance

Hypotenuse – The leg of a triangle opposite of a right angle

Parallel – Two or more identical, coplanar lines which share the same slope but never share a point

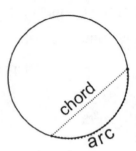

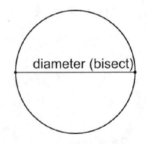

Perimeter – The distance around any enclosed two-dimensional figure

Perpendicular – Two coplanar lines which cross one another and form four 90° angles; the slopes of these lines will be negative reciprocals

Quadrilateral – Any enclosed, four-sided area (e.g., rectangle, rhombus, etc.)

Radius – The distance from the center of a circle to any point along the circumference.

Reflection

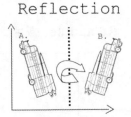

Reflection – To reflect across the x- or y-axis

Rotation

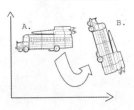

Rotation – To turn

Translation

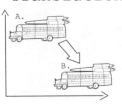

Translation – To slide

Volume – The space contained within a three-dimensional figure

Formulas to Remember

Perimeter: p = side$_1$ + side$_2$ + side$_3$ + …. side$_n$

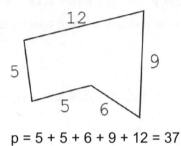

p = 5 + 5 + 6 + 9 + 12 = 37

Area of a Rectangle: A = Length × Width

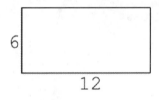

A = 6 x 12 = 72

Area of a Parallelogram: A = Base × Height

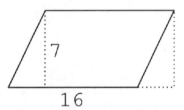

A = 7 x 16 = 112

Area of a Circle: A = π × r²

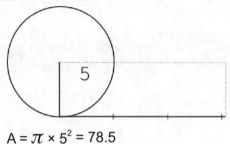

A = π × 5² = 78.5

Area of a Triangle: A = ½ × Base × Height

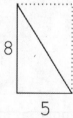

A = ½ x 5 x 8 = 20

Area of a Trapezoid: A = ½Height(base₁ + base₂)

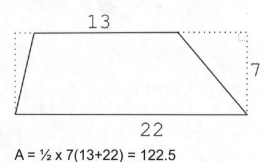

A = ½ x 7(13+22) = 122.5

formulas
TO REMEMBER

NOTES:

Volume of a Rectangular Solid: V = Length × Width × Height

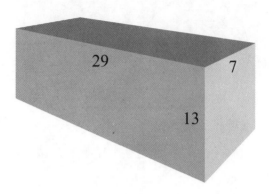

V = 29 x 7 x 13 = 2639

Pythagorean Theorem: For a right triangle, $a^2 + b^2 = c^2$

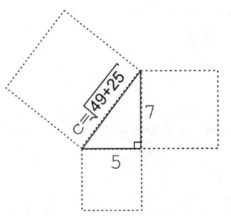

(c is the hypotenuse)

$a = 5 \qquad b = 7 \qquad c = \sqrt{49 + 25} = \sqrt{74}$

(also correct is $a = 7$, $b = 5$)

formulas
TO REMEMBER

NOTES:

Right Triangles

45-45-90° - The legs and hypotenuse are always in a ratio
of $1:1:\sqrt{2}$

30-60-90° - The legs and hypotenuse are always in a ratio
of $1:\sqrt{3}:2$

Pythagorean Triples are common side lengths that can
be memorized as right triangles. Pythagorean triples
include 3-4-5, 5-12-13, 8-15-17, 7-24-25, and 9-40-41
(and subsequent multiples of these combinations). The
right angle will be formed at the vertex of the two shorter
lengths.

Similar Triangles

Given two or more triangles specified as similar, a ratio may be
established to calculate a missing leg length.

If the below triangles are similar, find x.

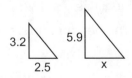

$$\frac{3.2}{2.5} = \frac{5.9}{x} \qquad x = (5.9)(2.5)/3.2 = 4.6$$

NOTES:

TRIGONOMETRY

SOH-CAH-TOA

This mnemonic has saved students since the terrible dawn of Trigonometry. SOH-CAH-TOA is a nice little acronym for the three base ratios: sine, cosine, and tangent. You can remember their identities thusly:

SOH: $\sin = \dfrac{\text{opposite}}{\text{hypotenuse}}$

CAH: $\cos = \dfrac{\text{adjacent}}{\text{hypotenuse}}$

TOA: $\tan = \dfrac{\text{opposite}}{\text{adjacent}}$

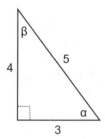

$\sin(\beta) = 3/5 \quad \cos(\beta) = 4/5 \quad \tan(\beta) = 3/4$

$\sin(\alpha) = 4/5 \quad \cos(\alpha) = 3/5 \quad \tan(\alpha) = 4/3$

The reciprocals of these identities (csc, sec, and cot) are obtained by swapping the numerator and denominator:

(Helpful little hint to remember the trigonometric functions and their reciprocals: tan & cot both have T's and sin/csc and cos/sec each have one S and one C. The one with the "co" goes with the one with no "co".)

formulas TO REMEMBER

Trigonometric Identities

Sorry, guys. These will just have to be memorized.

$$\sin^2 x + \cos^2 x = 1$$

$$\sin 2x = 2\sin x \cos x$$

$$\cos 2x = \cos^2 x - \sin^2 x$$

$$\tan 2x = \frac{2 \tan x}{1 - \tan^2 x}$$

And there is your high school math career! It might look like a lot, but it took you years to get through high school and only 69 pages to get through this chapter – so how about *them* cupcakes?

formulas TO REMEMBER

CALCULATOR LOVE

The worst way to waste time during the math section (other than making kissie faces at the cutie two desks over) is by fumbling blindly with your calculator in search of that pesky secant function. The second worst way is to use a calculator to perform basic computations that your brain could very well handle in a fraction of the time it takes your fingers to punch away at the keys. It's OK to love your calculator, but learn how to give it a rest and **put your brain into gear first.**

Tips to a healthy calculator relationship:

*   Spend some quality time with your calculator. As you do practice problems, take note of the location of frequently used keys—especially the second function button. A common mistake students make is forgetting how to access secondary key functions such as x10^y.

*   Even if your calculator does not report answers in fraction form, finding the value of your answer and the value of fractions listed as possible answers can save time. While a fraction problem may be calculable in the form of a fraction, it may simply take significantly longer to go through the steps. So find your answer and, using your brain, estimate which of the listed fractions may be close to your calculated answer. Plug those fraction(s) into your calculator and see which it is!

*   Know how to change your batteries and bring a fresh set. While all of the questions on the ACT can be answered without a calculator (after all, calculators didn't even exist in the ACT's early years), you would be at a great disadvantage if yours pooped out just two questions into the exam.

WHEN YOU'RE UNSURE...

If a question isn't obviously impossible (impossible as in, you've never taken Trigonometry and you're facing one of the four problems...and you didn't have the joy of reading this book), try one of these techniques before abandoning all hope—especially if you're on one of the earlier, easier problems:

Change Perspectives

Sometimes it only takes an alteration in your point of view to make a difficult problem easier than it is to fall victim to the internet's time-devouring maw (don't think about checking out your e-mail right now—this is business!). From restating the problem to re-drawing diagrams, altering your perspective can make the route to an answer jump out at you.

Simplify

So you turn the page and see a question that spans about five lines and includes two diagrams. You begin to wonder what you're supposed to learn in college if you're expected to know *this* before ever setting foot in a university. But wait, why do you need to know what Extractive Metallurgist Engineers do for a living? And why do we need to pay attention to the long percent composition list for this sample when we're only being asked to calculate the iron composition? De-fluff the question and simplify the problem at hand.

Tips

Work in Reverse

Sometimes a problem requires too much time to actually work it out. Since we know that the correct answer must be one of our five options, we can always deal with these questions by backsolving (i.e., plugging in the provided answers). For example:

If $8x + 3x + (x - 4) = 116$, then $x = ?$

> A. 3
> B. 5
> C. 8
> D. 10
> E. 13

Instead of taking the time to smoosh this monster into something a little more manageable, grab the *middle* value and plug it in. This first try will tell you if the middle number is correct or if your number needs to be larger or smaller. And since there will only be two other options, you'll only have to verify or eliminate one, thus helping you to solve the problem with only two tries!

If $x = 8$: $8(8) + 3(8) + (8 - 4) = 102$ Incorrect.

If $x = 10$: $8(10) + 3(10) + (10 - 4) = 116$ Correct!

Assign Numbers

If you're presented with an abstract problem—say, one referring to positive and negative integers—randomly pick numbers and substitute them into the problem. Try it with the following:

If x is a positive, odd integer and y is a negative, odd integer, which expression will result in a negative, even integer?

F. $2xy^2$

G. $3xy^3$

H. $2x^2y$

J. $3x^5y$

K. $3x^3y$

Instead of trying to wrap your brain around this abstract x and y business, assign values to each and test them out.

Let $x = +1$ and $y = -1$

F. $2(1)(-1)^2 = 2$

G. $3(1)(-1)^3 = -3$

H. $2(1)^2(-1) = -2$

J. $3(1)^5(-1) = -3$

K. $3(1)^3(-1) = -3$

After simplifying the problem by assigning numbers and checking the results, it's easy to see that only answer H provides us with a negative, even integer.

NOTES:

ADDITIONAL MATH TIPS

- Do a whole lot of scribbling in your test book. This includes labeling diagrams as information is collected and taking notes for your second pass. It's also helpful to do math on paper—not in your head—as writing it out decreases opportunity for silly errors and also provides information for your second-sweep (if necessary).

- Draw diagrams to help visualize the problem. This is especially helpful for questions that refer to a given object with x and y dimensions. Drawing the object with labels may simplify a problem that would otherwise stump you.

> An unframed painting is three times as long as it is wide. After being framed in a border two inches wide, the area of the framed painting becomes 1040 inches. How long is the painting?
>   A. 16"
>   B. 32"
>   C. 48"
>   D. 40"
>   E. Not enough information provided.

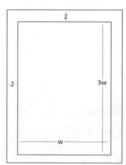

A quick sketch gives us the image to the left. Based on this, we know we're looking for an area of
$(3w + 2 + 2)(w + 2 + 2) = 1040$.
Distribute, set the equation equal to zero, and solve for w. If we find that w = 16, what is the length?

L = 3w, or 3(16) = 48 inches-answer C

Tips

- A diagram, even though the directions say that diagrams aren't necessarily drawn to scale, may be a huge clue for a question. If necessary, quickly redraw the diagram so that it is as close to scale as possible. Seek visual cues which, while they may not tell you the exact answer, may eliminate bad answers and increase your chances at a correct answer—especially if you're painfully short on time or have no idea how to do the calculation.

Imagine you're asked to determine which leg of the following triangle, x or y, is longer.

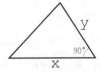

As shown, the diagram is not drawn to scale and the answer isn't obvious. However, if we redraw the diagram to correctly represent a 90° angle, it's easier to see that leg x is significantly longer than leg y.

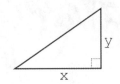

NOTES:

- Some questions may stump you initially, yet leave you with a lingering feeling of comprehension. For these problems, mark them in your test booklet and move on. During the last 15 to 25 minutes, perform a second pass over your exam and revisit those eerily familiar questions. Your mind may have fetched the information while you were consciously working on other questions (our brains are sneaky like that). If the second pass doesn't provide an "A*ha*" moment, make an educated guess and move on. But don't ever leave an unanswered question during this second pass! (We promise there won't be time for a third pass—don't plan for it.)

- The answer, not your route to the answer, is what matters. Guess-and-plug is sometimes better than taking the time to solve a problem. By cramming entirely too many questions into the math section, the ACT committee is analyzing your abilities as a swift, creative thinker and problem-solver.

think creatively!

Tips

• Some ACT questions will appear very difficult to solve when they are truly only a matter of discovering a pattern of sorts. Consider the following:

What is the 25th decimal place in the fraction $\frac{17}{444}$?

A. 3
B. 4
C. 6
D. 8
E. 9

Instead of carrying out the division, plug the fraction into your calculator. You should get back something along the lines of, "0.3863636364."

Even though the decimal terminates, based on the pattern we can deduce that the 4 is a matter of rounding.

So our pattern goes .38**636363**...

After the first two decimal places, our pattern follows the form:

odd decimal place = 6
even decimal place = 3

Since 25 is odd, we know the 25th decimal place will be 6, or C.

Tips

NOTES:

- Break down complex problems into simpler steps. A question may appear intimidating, but, if it can be simplified into two or more easier calculations, it isn't any more difficult than any one of the intermediate steps.

What is the area of the following figure?

F. 338
G. 348
H. 476
J. 481
K. 595

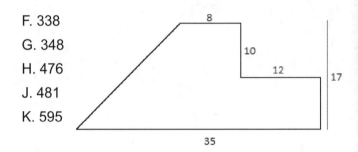

This problem becomes much more manageable if we draw in a few extra lines and label them.

Across the top we have lengths of 8 and 12, which gives us a total of 20. If the top section has a cumulative length 20 and the bottom length is a total of 35, the length of the left hand triangle must be equal to (35 – 20) 15.

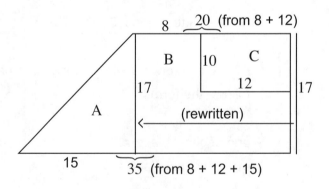

area of A + area of B - area of C
½(15 × 17) + (20 × 17) - (10 × 12) = 347.5

Rounded up to 348, the answer must be G.

- Carefully read questions before performing calculations. While a question may be solved with a complex computation, hints may exist in the question itself, which could save you a few precious seconds.

NOTES:

- <u>Underline</u> key phrases in the question. **Test Prep Alert:** Avoid the most common error on the ACT and know what is being asked of you. It's better to "waste" ten seconds reading than 60 seconds doing nonsense.

- Remember: **DRT**. **D**istance = **R**ate × **T**ime. This equation will definitely come in handy.

  Try this one out, for example:

  If Elizabeth sprints a distance of 2 miles in 10 minutes, how fast does she move?

  First, let's identify what we do and don't know.
  $D = 2$ miles $R = ?$ $T = 10$ minutes

  We then manipulate our equation to solve for our unknown which, in this case, is R.
  $D = R \times T$ $\rightarrow$ Dividing both sides by T: $D/T = R$

  Plugging in our values and solving:
  2 miles/10 minutes = R = 1 mile/5 minutes
  (or, in mph: 2mi / 10 min x 60 min/1 hr = 12 mph)

- There are a few numbers you may want to memorize in order to cut time: $\pi = 3.14$ $\sqrt{2} \approx 1.4$ $\sqrt{3} \approx 1.7$

Most of your points on this section will come from Algebra; so focus your energies there and make a point to frequent other branches of math. If you haven't already taken Trigonometry, don't fret; it's only worth approximately 4 points, anyway. And even though the other math may seem simple, it's important that you practice, and practice often. While the calculations may not be too difficult, the presentation may throw you off. Get accustomed to the problem types, know your math, and slap this section around with your pocket protector!

GOT THAT?

If nothing else...Check these out!

The math section of the ACT calls on topics from arithmetic to geometry and algebra. Don't panic! We've got you covered with 100 of the most tested concepts you'll see on the ACT.

Flip through this list to remind yourself of key topics you'll need to know. Pick five concepts a day, and you will be fully prepared in a month. Is there a concept that keeps tripping you up? Circle it, and refer to the page as you review your problems. You have probably learned this material in school already; so, this review should be a nice refresher.

Definitions

1. Numbers

A **prime number** is a number that only can be divided evenly by itself and by the number 1. For example, 7 is prime, because it can only be divided by 7 and by 1. However, 8 is not prime, because it can be divided by 1, 2, 4, and 8. Note that 1 and 0 are not prime numbers.

The **whole numbers** are the counting numbers, and they include zero: 0, 1, 2, 3, and so on.

An **integer** includes all whole numbers, but also includes negative numbers. Integers do not include any decimal parts or fractions.

An **irrational number** can't be expressed by a fraction, terminating decimal, or repeating decimal. For the ACT, the most important irrational numbers are $\sqrt{2}$, $\sqrt{3}$, and π.

2. Addition and Subtraction of Signed Numbers

When adding a positive and a negative number, first find the difference between them as if they were both positive. Then look to see whether the positive or the negative number part was larger to begin with. That is the sign the answer will have. So to add 18 and –25, you first find the difference between 25 and 18. 25 – 18 = 7. Now go back to check which was the larger number part originally: It was –25. So the answer will be negative, –7.

3. Multiplication and Division of Signed Numbers

Often you will multiply or divide signed numbers on your calculator. But one wrong keystroke can make an incorrect answer. Instead of including negatives and positives in the multiplication, multiply and divide the numbers as if they all were positive. **The answer will be negative if there is an odd number of negative multipliers or divisors.** For example, to multiply $-2 \times -3 \times -4$, multiply the number parts: $2 \times 3 \times 4 = 24$. Now count the negative signs in the original equation. There were three—an odd number—so the product is negative: $(-2) \times (-3) \times (-4) = -24$.

4. PEMDAS

Please Excuse My Dear Aunt Sally is the memory trick to remember the order of operations for simplifying a math expression. When you have multiple operations to do, follow the **PEMDAS** order: **Parentheses** first, then **Exponents**, followed by **Multiplication** and **Division** (from left to right), and finally **Addition** and **Subtraction** (from left to right).
To simplify the expression $3 \times (2 \times 5)^2 - 50 \times 4 + 200 \div 2$, we start with the parentheses: $(2 \times 5) = 10$.
Then we do the exponent: $(10)^2 = 100$, which gives us $3 \times 100 - 50 \times 4 + 200 \div 2$.
We do the multiplying and dividing next: $3 \times 100 = 300$, $-50 \times 4 = -200$, and $200 \div 2 = 100$.
At this point, the expression is: $300 - 200 + 100 = 200$

Number Operations

5. Arithmetic Sequences

A sequence that has a constant difference between the terms is an **arithmetic sequence**. The first term in the sequence is given as a_1, and each term that follows is a multiple of the constant difference. To find the nth term, use the formula $a_n = a_1 + (n - 1)d$ where a_n is the nth term, d is the common difference, and n is the number of the term you want. An example of an arithmetic sequence would be 5, 8, 11, 14, 17. In this case, $a_1 = 5$, and $d = 3$.

6. Geometric Series

On the ACT, they sometimes give you a series of numbers and ask for the nth term. Here is how you solve this kind of problem. Let r be the ratio between consecutive terms, let a_1 be the first term and a_n be the nth term (the one you're looking for). Then $a_n = a_1 r^{n-1}$. Sometimes they ask for the sum of the first n terms, or S_n. The sum is $S_n = \dfrac{a_1 - a_1 r^n}{1 - r}$.

7. Union and Intersection of Sets

The **union** of two sets is the combination of items that are in either one set or the other. The union of Set A and Set B is written as $A \cup B$. If Set A = {5, 7, 8} and Set B = {2, 5} then $A \cup B$ = {2, 5, 7, 8}. The **intersection** of Set A and Set B, written as $A \cap B$, means the items that the sets have in common. In this case, $A \cap B$ = {5}.

Factoring

8. Factors

The **factors** of an integer n are the positive integers that divide evenly into n. For example, the factors of 24 are 1, 2, 3, 4, 6, 8, 12, and 24.

9. Prime Factors

Finding the prime factors of a number means breaking down all the factors until only primes are left. When you multiply all the prime factors together, you should get the original number. In prime factorization, it is OK to list a factor more than once. For example, here is how to find the prime factor of 24.
$24 = 8 \times 3 = 2 \times 2 \times 2 \times 3$.

10. Useful Powers of 2

Knowing the values of the powers of 2 is a good way to solve problems. The value of $2^2 = 4$, and $2^3 = 8$. Can you quickly recognize that $2^4 = 16$, and $2^5 = 32$? These will come in handy for many different types of problems on the ACT.
Two more: $2^6 = 64$, and $2^7 = 128$.

11. Common Multiple

You sometimes will have to figure out the smallest common multiple of two numbers. This is also known as the least common denominator. Of course, two numbers multiplied together will give a product that both numbers divide into evenly. But we can make life easier by finding a smaller number that both of our numbers divide into evenly. For example, what is the smallest common multiple of 8 and 12? You could just multiply $8 \times 12 = 96$. To find the smallest common multiple, take multiples of the larger number until one is divisible by the smaller number. For our example, start with 12: 12 is not divisible by 8; 24 is divisible by 8, so it's the smallest common multiple.

12. Greatest Common Factor

The greatest common factor is the largest number that can divide evenly into two different numbers. A simple example is 8 and 12: The greatest common factor is 4. How do we determine this for larger numbers where the answer doesn't "jump out" at us? Break down each number using prime factorization, then multiply all the prime factors they have in common. For example, using 36 and 48: $36 = 2 \times 2 \times 3 \times 3$, and $48 = 2 \times 2 \times 2 \times 2 \times 3$. The common prime factors are two 2s and one 3. So, the greatest common factor is $2 \times 2 \times 3 = 12$.

13. Even and Odd Factors and Sums

For double-checking or just eliminating answers, figuring out whether the answer should be even or odd is a handy trick. For example, any odd number multiplied by an even number will have an even result. This is a little challenging to memorize. So, a better way is to try simple numbers such as 1 and 2 and see what happens. This is useful for predicting whether a sum, difference, or product should be even or odd.

14. Multiples of 2 and 4

Recognizing divisibility is a good way to turn a 3-minute problem into a 30-second problem. You know a number is divisible by 2 if the last digit is divisible by 2, or in other words, if the number is even. What about divisibility by 4? Just look at the last two digits. If the number formed by the last two digits is divisible by 4, then the entire number, no matter how many digits it has, is also divisible by 4. For example, the number 516 is even. So, it is divisible by 2. The last two digits, 16, form a number that is divisible by 4. So 516 is divisible by 4.

15. Multiples of 3 and 9

Finding out if a number is divisible by 3 or 9 is as easy as adding up the digits of the number. If the sum of the digits is divisible by 3, then the number is divisible by 3. If the sum of the digits is divisible by 9, then the number is divisible by 9. For example, the sum of the digits in 951 is 15, which is divisible by 3, but not divisible by 9; so 951 is divisible by 3, but not by 9.

16. Multiples of 5 and 10

Integers whose last digit is 5 or 0 are divisible by 5. Integers whose last digit is 0 are divisible by 10. For example, 755 is divisible by 5, but not by 10.

17. Remainder

The **remainder** is the number left over when one number does not divide into another number evenly. For example, 456 is 1 more than 455, which 5 divides into evenly; so, when 456 is divided by 5, the remainder is 1.

Fractions and Decimals

18. Reducing Fractions

To reduce a fraction, factor the top and bottom parts and cancel out all common factors.

$$\frac{40}{55} = \frac{5 \times 8}{5 \times 11} = \frac{8}{11}$$

19. Addition and Subtraction of Fractions

When adding or subtracting fractions, the first step is to find a common denominator. Next, add or subtract the numerators.

$$\frac{5}{8} - \frac{7}{12} = \frac{15}{24} - \frac{14}{24} = \frac{15 - 14}{24} = \frac{1}{24}$$

20. Multiplication of Fractions

When multiplying fractions, multiply the numerators together, and multiply the denominators together.

$$\frac{3}{7} \times \frac{5}{8} = \frac{3 \times 5}{7 \times 8} = \frac{15}{56}$$

21. Division of Fractions

When dividing fractions, invert the second fraction and then multiply.

$$\frac{2}{3} \div \frac{1}{2} = \frac{2}{3} \times \frac{2}{1} = \frac{2 \times 2}{3 \times 1} = \frac{4}{3}$$

22. Improper Fractions and Mixed Numbers

Answers on the ACT may be given as improper fractions (which give an amount larger than one, such as $\frac{4}{3}$) or as mixed numbers (such as $1\frac{1}{3}$). It is important to recognize when you have found the correct answer, but the answer choice is in another form. To convert an improper fraction to a mixed number, divide the numerator by the denominator to get a whole number with a remainder. The remainder is the new numerator for the fraction.

For example, if you have

$$\frac{225}{8}$$

then to convert it to a mixed number, divide 225 by 8. The result is 28 with a remainder of 1. This gives a mixed number of

$$28\frac{1}{8}$$

To convert a mixed number to an improper fraction, multiply the whole number part by the denominator and add that amount to the numerator. For example, to convert $5\frac{1}{3}$ to an improper fraction, first multiply $5 \times 3 = 15$ and add that to the 1 from the numerator. The improper fraction is then

$$\frac{16}{3}$$

23. Reciprocal

The reciprocal of a fraction is found by swapping the numerator and the denominator. The reciprocal of $\frac{2}{3}$ is $\frac{3}{2}$. The reciprocal of 7 is $\frac{1}{7}$. Multiplying a fraction by its reciprocal gives a value of 1.

24. Comparing Fractions

Sometimes it is necessary to determine which of two fractions is larger. This can be a challenge if the fractions are not ones we use every day. One solution is to express both fractions with a common denominator. For example, compare $\frac{3}{5}$ and $\frac{5}{7}$.

$$\frac{3}{5} = \frac{21}{35} \text{ and } \frac{5}{7} = \frac{25}{35}$$

So $\frac{5}{7}$ is bigger than $\frac{3}{5}$. Another way to compare is to convert both fractions to decimals. $\frac{3}{5}$ converts to 0.6, and $\frac{5}{7}$ converts to approximately 0.714.

25. Identifying Addition and Subtraction

Word problems count for one-third of all questions on the math portion of the ACT. Your job is to turn these "stories" into equations with knowns and unknowns. Words such as "increase," "sum," "exceeds," "more than," and "is greater than by" mean **addition**. Words such as "less than" indicate **subtraction**. For example, "The number of students in Homeroom 1 exceeds the number of students in Homeroom 2 by 5."

X = Homeroom 2 students $X + 5 = Y$ = Homeroom 1 students

26. Identifying Multiplication and Division

The words "product," "times," and "of" mean multiplication in word problems. The words "a ratio of" signify division. For example, "The product of two numbers is also equal to a ratio of 3 to 4." The word "product" tells us two numbers are going to be multiplied, and the word "ratio" means 3 will be divided by 4.

$$X \times Y = \frac{3}{4}$$

27. Identifying the Parts and the Whole

The ACT will give you word problems where it is your job to identify the **part** and the **whole**. Usually this will be given in a phrase such as "Half of the girls are eight years old," where the word associated with "of" is the whole; and the word associated with the verb "is" (or it could be "are") is the part. For this example, the whole is the girls ("*of* the girls") and the part is those who are eight years old ("*are* eight years old").

Percent

28. Percent Formula

You will encounter many problems involving percent on the ACT, but they all use the same formula:

$$\text{Percent} = \frac{\text{Part}}{\text{Whole}}$$

For example, "What is 5 percent of 80?"

$$0.05 = \frac{\text{Part}}{80}$$

And for another example, "15 is 10 percent of what number?"

$$0.10 = \frac{15}{\text{Whole}}$$

One last example, "6 is what percent of 50?"

$$\text{Percent} = \frac{6}{50}$$

29. Percent Increase and Percent Decrease

To increase a number by a percent, use this method. Add the percent increase to 100 percent, convert to a decimal, and multiply by the original number. For example, "Increase 30 by 25 percent." First, add 25 percent to 100 percent, to get 125 percent. Convert 125 percent to a decimal by dividing 125 by 100, $125 \div 100 = 1.25$. Now multiply 1.25 by the original number, 30, $1.25 \times 30 = 37.5$. The method is the same for a percent decrease, except that you subtract the percent change from 100 in the first step.

NOTES:

30. Find the Whole

In order to find the original whole, before a percent increase or decrease, use this method. Set up an equation where the variable you will find is the whole. For example, "After a 10 percent increase, the number of home runs for the team was 198 for the season. What was the number of home runs before the increase?" A 10 percent increase is the same as 1.1 times the whole. The equation to describe this situation is $1.1x = 198$.

31. Multiple Changes in Percent

When given a problem that asks you to increase and decrease "a number" by some percent or a chain of percents, use 100 as a starting point to figure out what will happen. The test writers expect you to add and subtract the percents, but this will give you the wrong answer. For example, "A number is increased by 80 percent and then decreased by 50 percent. What is the ratio of the new number to the original number?" Starting with 100 percent and adding 80 percent gives us 180 percent. Decreasing 180 percent by 50 percent gives us 90 percent. The new number is 90 percent, and the original number was 100 percent, so the ratio of new/original is 90/100.

Ratios, Proportions, and Rates

32. Setting Up a Ratio

In word problems, a ratio is often set up as "a ratio of x to y." To set up the ratio mathematically, set the number closest to the word "of" on the top, and set the number closest to the word "to" on the bottom. For example: "The ratio of 30 oranges to 40 apples." This is expressed as 30/40, which can be reduced to 3/4.

33. Part-to-Whole Ratios

Sometimes, an ACT math problem gives you a part-to-part ratio, and your job is to turn it into two part-to-whole ratios. This is possible—if the parts add up to the whole. To find a part-to-whole ratio, put one part in the top of the ratio, and put the sum of all the parts in the bottom of the ratio. For example, "The ratio of dogs to cats in the neighborhood is 2 to 3. What is the overall ratio of dogs to all pets?" Since there are 2 dogs, and the total of dogs plus cats is 2 + 3 = 5, the ratio of dogs to all pets is 2/5. In other words, 2/5 of all pets in the neighborhood are dogs.

34. Solving a Proportion

Solving proportions involves two steps: (1) write down the proportion based on the word problem; and (2) cross multiply to solve. For example, "There are 30.48 centimeters in 12 inches. How many centimeters are there in 20 inches?" The ratio is $\frac{12}{30.48} = \frac{20}{x}$. Cross-multiplying gives us $12x = 20 \times 30.48$, or $x = \frac{20 \times 30.48}{12}$.

35. Rates

Rate problems always use the formula $D = RT$ or Distance = Rate × Time. Use the units to double-check your answers. For example, "The butterfly flew across the lake at a rate of 20 feet per minute. The lake was 850 feet across. How long did it take for the butterfly to cross the lake?" Rearranged, the formula is $T = D/R$. Time = 850 feet / 20 feet per minute. The units cancel out and answer the problem in minutes for the time.

36. Average Rate

Never take two rates and take the average of them—this is an all-too-common mistake. To find an average rate, divide the total distance by the total time. For example, "What is the average speed for a trip where one leg went 60 miles at 30 miles per hour, and the second leg went 200 miles at 50 miles per hour?" The total distance is 60 miles + 200 miles = 260 miles. The total time is 2 hours + 4 hours = 6 hours. The average speed is 260 / 6 = 43.33 miles per hour.

Averages

37. Average Formula

The formula for the average is known as the TAN formula, Total = Average × Number. The total is the sum of the values, and the number is how many values there were. For example, "What is the average of the numbers 6, 17, 20, 21, and 21?" First, the total is $T = 6 + 17 + 20 + 21 + 21 = 85$. The number $N = 5$. $T = A \times N$, $85 = A \times 5$, $A = 17$.

38. Average of Evenly Spaced Numbers

To find the average of numbers that are evenly spaced, we can save time by averaging just the largest and smallest values. For example, "What is the average of all integers from 10 to 72?" From our TAN formula, Average = Total / Number = $(10 + 72) / 2 = 82/2 = 41$.

By the way, another math term for "average" is "mean"

39. Using the Average to Find the Total

Using the TAN formula, the total can be found by using the average and the number of terms. For example, "If the average of 5 numbers is 40, what is their total?" From the TAN formula, Total = Average × Number = $40 \times 5 = 200$.

40. Median

The median is the middle value of a set of numbers, when the numbers are in order. For example, "What is the median of the following five test scores: 72, 83, 92, 90, 81?" First, rearrange the numbers in increasing or decreasing order: 72, 81, 83, 90, 92. Now it is clear that the middle value is 83.

What if the number of items in the set is even? In that case, take the average of the two middle values.

41. Mode

The mode is the number in a set that occurs most frequently. For example, "What is the mode of the following set: 44, 46, 50, 44, 60, 88, 30? Since 44 occurs twice and all other numbers appear just once, the mode is 44.

Combinations and Probability

42. Combinations

To figure out how many combinations are possible, multiply the number of *m* ways for one event to happen by the number of *n* ways for the other event to happen. That gives us *m* × *n* ways for the two events to happen. For example, "John has 5 shirts and 3 pairs of pants. How many different combinations can he wear?" In this case, John has 5 × 3 = 15 different outfits.

43. Probability

Probability is a part-to-whole ratio. The top part is the number of desirable outcomes, and the bottom part is the total number of outcomes possible.

$$\text{Probability} = \frac{\text{Desirable Outcomes}}{\text{Total Possible Outcomes}}$$

For example, "There are 14 blue socks and 6 red socks in the drawer. What is the probability of picking a blue sock at random?" The desirable outcome is picking a blue sock, or 14. The total possible outcomes are 14 + 6 = 20. The probability is 14/20 = 7/10. This probability also can be expressed as 0.7 or 70 percent.

Exponents

44. Multiplying and Dividing Exponents

For exponents of the same base multiplied together, **add the exponents.**

$$x^2 \times x^5 = x^{2+5} = x^7$$

For exponents of the same base that are divided, **subtract the exponents.**

$$\frac{y^{10}}{y^3} = y^{10-3} = y^7$$

45. Exponents Raised to an Exponent

When an exponent is raised to an exponent power, multiply the exponents.

$$\left(x^3\right)^2 = x^{3 \times 2} = x^6$$

46. Simplifying Square Roots

Any perfect square that factors within a square root can be unsquared and removed from the square root sign.

$$\sqrt{50} = \sqrt{25 \times 2} = \sqrt{5 \times 5 \times 2} = \sqrt{5 \times 5} \times \sqrt{2} = 5\sqrt{2}$$

47. Adding and Subtracting Roots

If the value under the radical is the same, radical expressions can be added and subtracted.

$$4\sqrt{5} + 5\sqrt{5} = 9\sqrt{5}$$

However, if the value under the radical is not the same, then you can't simplify by adding and subtracting. The following expression can't be simplified:

$$6\sqrt{3} + 2\sqrt{5}$$

48. Multiplying and Dividing Roots

The square root of one value multiplied by the square root of another value may be combined as multiples under the same square root sign.

$$\sqrt{5} \times \sqrt{11} = \sqrt{5 \times 11} = \sqrt{55}$$

When both parts of a fraction are within a square root sign, each part may be set in its own square root sign.

$$\frac{\sqrt{6}}{\sqrt{2}} = \sqrt{\frac{6}{2}} = \sqrt{3}$$

NOTES:

You also can get the radical out of the bottom part of a fraction by multiplying both the top and bottom parts by the bottom radical. This is the same as multiplying a fraction by 1.

$$\frac{1}{\sqrt{2}} \times \frac{\sqrt{2}}{\sqrt{2}} = \frac{\sqrt{2}}{\sqrt{2 \times 2}} = \frac{\sqrt{2}}{2}$$

It will save you time if you memorize the value 0.7071 for the decimal value of this expression.

49. Negative Exponents and Fractional Exponents

Negative exponents indicate that the value can be thought of as the reciprocal of the positive exponent.

$$3^{-2} = \frac{1}{3^2} = \frac{1}{9}$$

Fractional exponents are the same as roots. A square root can also be written as a base raised to the 1/2 power. A cube root can also be written as a base raised to the 1/3 power.

$$\sqrt{2} = 2^{1/2}$$

An exponent in the form of $\frac{a}{b}$ means that the base is raised to the a power and also raised to the $\frac{1}{b}$ power, or in other words, to the b root.

$$4^{3/2} = 64^{1/2} = \sqrt{64} = 8$$

Absolute Value

50. Absolute Value

The absolute value of a number can be thought of as the distance from the number to zero on the number line. This distance is never negative. The absolute value of 5 is 5. Another way to put this is $|5| = 5$. The absolute value of –5 is also 5, $|-5| = 5$.

Algebraic Terms

51. Plug and Chug

Evaluating an algebraic expression can be done by plugging in the value for the variable, and chugging through the equation to find the value of the expression. For example, "What is the value of $2x^2 + x + 5$ if $x = -3$?" First, plug in the value of -3 for x.

$$2(-3)^2 + (-3) + 5 = 2(9) - 3 + 5 = 18 - 3 + 5 = 20$$

52. Adding and Subtracting Like Terms

Be careful when combining like terms. Make sure to add and subtract the coefficients of terms that are alike. For example, "What is the simplified way to show $3a + 2b - a + 5b$?" First, rewrite the expressions with the like terms grouped together.

$$3a + 2b - a + 5b = 3a - a + 2b + 5b$$
$$= 2a + 7b$$

53. Adding and Subtracting Polynomials

When adding and subtracting polynomials, there is more variety in what the variables may look like, but this is really just the same method: **group like terms, then add and subtract the coefficients**. For example, "What is a simplified view of the expression $(2x^2 - 3x + 14) - (x^2 + 7)$?" First, we rewrite the equation with the minus sign applied to the second parenthetic term.

$$(2x^2 - 3x + 14) - (x^2 + 7)$$
$$= 2x^2 - 3x + 14 - x^2 - 7$$
$$= 2x^2 - x^2 - 3x + 14 - 7$$
$$= x^2 - 3x + 7$$

54. Multiplying Monomials

To multiply monomials, multiply the coefficients together, and multiply the variables together. For example, "What is the simplified way to show $3x \times 4x$?" First multiply the coefficients (3×4). Then multiply the variables $(x \times x)$.

$$3x \times 4x = (3 \times 4)(x \times x) = 12x^2$$

55. FOIL—Multiplying Binomials

FOIL is another memory trick, this one for remembering how to multiply binomials. To multiply the binomial $(x + 2)$ by $(x + 5)$, use the FOIL method to multiply the **F**irst terms: $x \times x = x^2$.
Next multiply the **O**uter terms: $x \times 5 = 5x$.
Next, the **I**nner terms: $2 \times x = 2x$.
Finally, multiply the **L**ast terms: $2 \times 5 = 10$.
The last step is to combine like terms:
$(x + 2)(x + 5) = x^2 + 5x + 2x + 10 = x^2 + 7x + 10$.

56. Multiplying Polynomials in General

FOIL is useful when multiplying binomials, but sometimes we have to multiply polynomials with more terms. Just multiply each term in the first polynomial by each term in the second polynomial, group like terms together, and simplify. For example, "What is the simplified way to show $(2x^2 + x - 3)(x + 4)$?"

$$(2x^2 + x - 3)(x + 4) =$$
$$2x^2(x + 4) + x(x + 4) - 3(x + 4) =$$
$$2x^3 + 8x^2 + x^2 + 4x - 3x - 12$$
$$= 2x^3 + 9x^2 + x - 12$$

Factoring Algebraic Expressions

57. Factoring Out a Common Factor

If there is a factor common to all terms, it can be factored out of a polynomial. For example, "Completely factor the following expression, $6x^3 + 12x^2 - 6x$." For this expression, each term has a common factor of $6x$ that can be factored out.

$$6x^3 + 12x^2 - 6x = 6x(x^2 + 2x - 1).$$

58. Factoring the Difference of Squares

You can count on seeing a case of factoring the difference of squares in the math section.

$$a^2 - b^2 = (a + b)(a - b)$$

The important clue you will get is that both terms are squares, so be watchful of the perfect square numbers: 1, 4, 9, 16, 25, 36, 49, 64, 81, and 100, for the squares of the numbers 1 through 10. For example, "Factor $x^2 - 16$." $x^2 - 16 = (x + 4)(x - 4)$.

59. Factoring the Square of a Binomial

Learn to recognize polynomials that are the square of a binomial. With a little practice, you will be able to spot these.

$$(a + b)^2 = a^2 + 2ab + b^2$$
$$(a - b)^2 = a^2 - 2ab + b^2$$

For example, "Factor $4x^2 + 12xy + 9y^2$." The center term is positive, so we are looking for the $(a + b)^2$ type. Using the first formula, $4x^2 + 12xy + 9y^2$ factors to $(2x + 3y)^2$.

For another example, "Factor $z^2 - 10z + 25$." The negative sign in front of the second term tells us we are looking at the $(a - b)^2$ type. Using the second formula, $z^2 - 10z + 25$ factors to $(z - 5)^2$.

60. Factoring Binomials from Quadratic Expressions

With practice, you can recognize a quadratic expression that is really a multiple of binomials. Factoring out binomials is like doing the FOIL process in reverse. For example, "Factor the quadratic expression $2x^2 + 7x + 3$." What two **F**irst terms multiplied together could give the term $2x^2$? The first terms of the binomials will be $2x$ and x. What are the factors of the last term? The **L**ast terms will be 3 and 1. Combine the first terms and last terms one way and another, until the combined **O**uter and **I**nner terms add up to $7x$, and you will see that

$2x^2 + 7x + 3 = (x + 3)(2x + 1)$.

61. Simplifying Algebraic Fractions

Just like simplifying a fraction with only numbers, simplifying algebraic fractions follows the method of canceling out common factors from the numerator and the denominator. The first step will be to factor the expressions.

For example, "Simplify the following fraction."

$$\frac{x^2 - 3x - 4}{x^2 - 8x + 16}$$

First factor the numerator and the denominator.

$$\frac{x^2 - 3x - 4}{x^2 - 8x + 16} = \frac{(x + 1)(x - 4)}{(x - 4)^2}$$

Canceling the factor of $(x - 4)$ from the numerator and the denominator leaves the simplified

$$\frac{(x + 1)}{(x - 4)}$$

Solving Equations

62. Solving an Equation: One Variable

The math test may present you with an expression that includes an equals sign. To solve this type of problem, group the variable terms on one side of the equals sign, and the other terms on the other side. For example, "Find the value of x in the following equation $3x + 4 = x - 2$." First, rearrange the terms, $3x - x = -2 - 4$. Simplify both sides, $2x = -6$. Next, divide both sides by 2, $x = -3$.

63. Solving an Equation: Two Variables

When you have an equation with two different variables, the first step is to solve for one variable in terms of the other variable. This means separating the variables on either side of the equals sign. For example, "Solve the following equation for m in terms of t: $3m + 5t = t - 5m$." First, move the variables to opposite sides of the equals sign, $3m + 5m = t - 5t$, or $8m = -4t$. Divide both sides by 8: $m = -1/2t$.

64. Substituting Values into Linear Equations

Solving a pair of linear equations requires us to solve for one variable in terms of another. The next step is to substitute the value of the first variable from one equation into the second equation. This results in an equation that has gone from two variables down to one variable. For example, "Find the value of x in the expression $x = 3y + 2$, by substituting the value of $y = 4x - 1$."

$$x = 3y + 2 = 3(4x - 1) + 2 = 12x - 3 + 2$$
$$x - 12x = -3 + 2$$
$$-11x = -1$$
$$x = 1/11$$

65. Solving a Quadratic Equation

A quadratic equation should be set up in the form of $ax^2 + bx + c = 0$. By doing this, factoring the quadratic equation (if it is possible) can give us the two solutions of the quadratic equation. In this process, set each of the factors equal to zero and solve for x. For example, "Find the solutions of the quadratic equation $x^2 - 4x - 12 = 0$." Our first task is to factor the expression $x^2 - 4x - 12 = (x + 2)(x - 6)$. By setting each factored part to zero, we find the solutions, $x + 2 = 0$, and $x - 6 = 0$. The solutions are then $x = -2$ and $x = 6$.

66. Solving a System of Equations

A second way to solve a pair of linear equations is to add the two equations together in such a way that one variable is eliminated. To do this, the equations must be rearranged so that one variable matches up in both equations. For example, "Solve the following two equations, $5x + 3y = 4$ and $x + y = 6$." Multiply each side of the second equation by 5 to match the first equation. $5x + 5y = 30$.

$$
\begin{array}{r}
5x + 3y = 4 \\
-(5x + 5y = 30) \\
\hline
-2y = -26 \\
y = 13
\end{array}
$$

Finally, substitute the value of $y = 13$ into one of the equations to find a value of $x = -7$.

67. Solving an Inequality

Some expressions can use an inequality instead of an equals sign. To solve an inequality, just as with equations with an equals sign, isolate the variable on one side. The only difference to note is that **any time both sides are multiplied or divided by a negative number, the inequality must be reversed**. For example, "Solve the inequality $-3x + 2 \leq -7$ for x." First, isolate the variable on one side. $-3x \leq -7 - 2$, which is equivalent to $-3x \leq -9$. The final step is to divide both sides by -3. Since you have divided both sides by a negative number, remember to reverse the sign: $x \geq 3$.

68. Equations with Radical Terms

A variable in a radical can seem intimidating, but just treat it as you would any variable: isolate it, and square both sides to spring the variable out of the radical. For example, "Solve $5\sqrt{x} + 4 = 24$ for x." Isolating the variable on one side gives $5\sqrt{x} = 20$; dividing both sides by 5 gives us $\sqrt{x} = 4$. Squaring both sides solves the equation: $x = 16$.

Functions

69. Evaluating Functions

Function notation is written as $f(x)$, which is read as "function of x" or simply "f of x." To evaluate the function $f(x) = 3x + 5$ for $f(2)$, substitute x with 2 and simplify, $f(2) = 3(2) + 5 = 6 + 5 = 11$.

70. Direct Variation and Inverse Variation

In a direct variation, one term increases as another term increases. The general form of a direct variation is $y = kx$, where k is a constant that does not equal zero. For example, if a phone plan gives 50 minutes for every dollar paid, this can be expressed as $D = 50m$. If the number of minutes used were to double, then the amount of dollars will double also.

In an inverse relationship, as one term increases, the other term decreases proportionally. For example, the DRT formula, Distance = Rate × Time, shows an inverse relationship between rate and time if distance is constant. As the rate is doubled, the time is divided by two.

71. Domain and Range of a Function

The domain of a function is the allowed inputs to a function, and the range of the function is the set of all values that may be outputs of a function. When asked to give the domain for a function, it is important to look into what values will not allow it to be evaluated. For example, "What is the domain of the function $f(x) = 1/(1 - x)$?" The denominator of a fraction is not allowed to equal zero. So, a value of x that would make the denominator be zero is not in the range. $1 - x = 0$ when $x = 1$. Therefore, the domain of the function is all numbers not equal to 1.

The range of a function such as $f(x) = x^2 + 1$ is all numbers greater than or equal to 1, because x^2 cannot have a negative value.

Coordinate Geometry

72. Distance Between Two Points in the Coordinate Plane

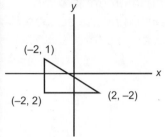

There are two ways to find the distance between two points in the coordinate plane. One way is to use the **Pythagorean Theorem**, and the other is to use the **distance formula**. The triangle can be drawn in the coordinate plane by dropping a vertical leg showing the y distance between the points, and drawing a horizontal line showing the x distance between the points. For example, "Find the distance between the points (−2, 1) and (2, −2)." Drawing these points on the coordinate axis, as shown in the figure, shows that the vertical leg is 3 and the horizontal leg is 4. Just knowing this, we can recognize it is a 3-4-5 triangle, and the distance between the two points is 5. Even without this insight, we can use the Pythagorean Theorem to find the third leg, $3^2 + 4^2 = x^2$ to again find that $x = 5$.

The distance formula can also be used

$$d = \sqrt{(x_1 - x_2)^2 + (y_1 - y_2)^2}$$

To find the distance between points (−2, 1) and (2, −2),

$$d = \sqrt{(-2 - 2)^2 + (1 - (-2))^2} = \sqrt{16 + 9} = \sqrt{25} = 5$$

73. Finding the Slope by Using Two Points

The slope is equal to the rise divided by the run, or the change in y divided by the change in x. For example, "Find the slope of a line that includes the points (1, 4) and (−3, 0)." The change in y is given by $4 - 0 = 4$. The change in x is given by $1 - (-3) = 4$. The rise divided by the run is 4/4 or 1.

74. Finding the Slope by Using the Equation of a Line

The equation describing a line is given in slope-intercept form as $y = mx + b$. The slope is m and the intercept is b. For example, "What is the slope of the line defined by the equation $2y - 6x - 10 = 0$?" First, rearrange the equation into $y = mx + b$ form.

$$2y - 6x - 10 = 0$$
$$y - 3x - 5 = 0$$
$$y = 3x + 5$$

The slope is 3.

75. Finding an Intercept by Using the Equation of a Line

The y-intercept is the place where a line crosses the y-axis. Using the slope-intercept form of a line, $y = mx + b$, the b is the y-intercept. Note that the y-intercept is the point where $x = 0$. This suggests another way to find the y-intercept is to set $x = 0$ and solve the equation for y. If you have to find the x-intercept, just set $y = 0$ and solve the equation for x.

Lines and Angles

76. Intersecting Lines

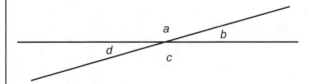

When two lines intersect, as in the figure, angles $\angle a$ and $\angle b$ are **supplementary angles**, which means that $\angle a + \angle b = 180°$. Angles $\angle a$ and $\angle c$ are **vertical angles**, which means that $\angle a = \angle c$. From these two facts, if you know one of the angles $\angle a$, $\angle b$, $\angle c$, or $\angle d$, then you can figure out the values of the other three angles.

For example, "If $\angle b = 20°$, what are the values of $\angle c$ and $\angle d$?"
Since $\angle b$ and $\angle d$ are vertical angles, then they are equal. So
$\angle b = \angle d = 20°$. Since $\angle b$ and $\angle c$ are supplementary angles,
$\angle b$ and $\angle c = 180°$, $= \angle c + 20° = 180°$, so $\angle c = 160°$.

NOTES:

77. Parallel Lines and Transversals

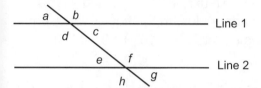

A transversal is a line that crosses two parallel lines, as in the
figure. Once you know any one angle of the angles formed,
you can figure out the others. The acute (less than 90°) angles
are all equal, and the obtuse (greater than 90°) angles are
all equal. In fact, any of the acute angles is supplementary
to any of the obtuse angles. For example, "Which angles are
supplementary to $\angle a$?" Angles $\angle b$, $\angle d$, $\angle f$, and $\angle h$ are
supplementary to $\angle a$. Corresponding angles are angles that
are in the same relative position to the transversal and the
parallel lines. For example, in the figure above, $\angle a$ and $\angle e$ are
corresponding angles. So are $\angle d$ and $\angle h$, $\angle b$ and $\angle f$,
and $\angle c$ and $\angle g$. By definition, corresponding angles are equal.

Triangles

78. Exterior and Interior Angles of a Triangle

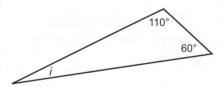

The sum of the angles of any triangle is 180°. In the figure, $\angle i$
is unknown, but the other two angles are given. So we know
that $\angle i + 110° + 60° = 180°$. This means that $\angle i = 10°$.

What else adds up to 180°? Supplementary angles! If we extend one line of the triangle, it forms an exterior angle of the triangle, shown as $\angle j$ in the figure. The exterior angle of a triangle is equal to the sum of the remote interior angles. In the figure, $\angle j$ is equal to the sum of the remote angles, or $\angle j = 110° + 60° = 170°$.

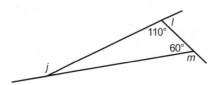

Another exterior angle tip is that the sum of all three exterior angles of any triangle is 360°. In the figure, $\angle j + \angle l + \angle m = 360°$.

79. Similar Triangles

Two triangles that have the same shape are similar triangles. For similar triangles, the corresponding angles are equal. Also, the corresponding sides are proportional to each other.

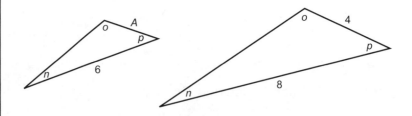

The triangles in the figure are similar because their angles measure the same. The sides are proportional. So to figure out the length of side A, we set up the proportion

$$\frac{A}{4} = \frac{6}{8}$$

$$A = 3.$$

80. Area of a Triangle

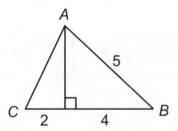

The formula for the area of a triangle is $A = 1/2bh$. That is, the area = 1/2 (base)(height). The height of a triangle is the length from the base to the opposite vertex. For example, "What is the area of triangle ABC?" In the figure, the base of triangle ABC is side CB, or 6. Since triangle ABC is not a right triangle, we need to draw a perpendicular line from side CB to point A. From the figure, the height of side h is 3. The area of the triangle is

$$A = \frac{1}{2}bh = \frac{1}{2} \times 6 \times 3 = 9$$

81. Triangle Properties

The sum of two sides must be greater than the length of the third side. Also, the difference of two sides must be less than the third side. If you are figuring out the third side of a triangle, you can use these checks to see if your answer is reasonable. For example, if two sides of a triangle are 8 and 11, the third side must be greater than 11 − 8, and less than 11 + 8.

82. Isosceles and Equilateral Triangles

An isosceles triangle is one with two equal sides. The angles opposite these sides are also equal. These angles are called the base angles.

Equilateral triangles have three equal sides and three equal angles. In fact, the three angles are all 60° angles.

Right Triangles

83. Pythagorean Theorem

Right triangles are triangles that have a right angle, or a 90° angle. The Pythagorean Theorem states that, for all right triangles, the length of the sides is given as $A^2 + B^2 = C^2$, where A and B are the two legs, and C is the hypotenuse. For example, "Find the length of the hypotenuse if the legs are $A = 5$ and $B = 12$." From the Pythagorean Theorem, $A^2 + B^2 = C^2$, so $5^2 + 12^2 = 25 + 144 = 169$. This means that $C^2 = 169$. Taking the square root of both sides gives us $C = 13$.

84. The 3-4-5 Triangle

Any right triangle with two legs that are 3 and 4 will have a hypotenuse of 5. If a right triangle has a leg of 4 and a hypotenuse of 5, then the other leg is 3. The 3-4-5 triangle can also show up on the ACT as any multiple of those sides, such as 6-8-10 (sides multiplied by two), or 9-12-15 (sides multiplied by three).

85. Turning Equilateral Triangles into Two Right Triangles

Since equilateral triangles have three 60° angles, they can be turned into two 30-60-90 triangles by drawing a perpendicular line from one side to the opposite vertex.

86. The 30-60-90 Triangle

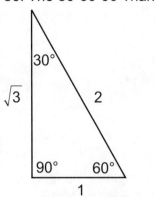

If you have a triangle with angles of 30°, 60°, and 90°, there are some shorthand ways to remember the leg lengths. The short leg is half of the hypotenuse. The hypotenuse is the short leg multiplied by 2. From the figure, you can also think of a 30-60-90 triangle as a $1 : \sqrt{3} : 2$ triangle. For example, if you have a right triangle where one base is half the hypotenuse, you know that it is a 30-60-90 triangle and that the second leg is $\sqrt{3}$ times the first leg.

87. The 45-45-90 Triangle

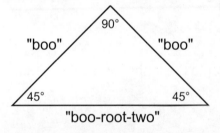

The isosceles right triangle, or the 45-45-90 triangle, is one to remember. If you know one of the leg lengths, then of course you know both leg lengths (because all isosceles triangles, even right ones, have equal leg lengths). The hypotenuse of this triangle equals the leg length multiplied by $\sqrt{2}$. The rounded off decimal of $\sqrt{2}$ is 1.414, for a quick calculation. The easy way to remember this is the saying, "boo, boo, boo-root-two," which means that if the leg length is "boo" then multiply the "boo" by "root two" ($\sqrt{2}$) to find the hypotenuse.

Other Polygons

88. Rectangle Properties

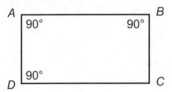

A rectangle is a four-sided figure with right angles. The lengths of the diagonals are equal. The long sides are equal and the short sides are equal. The perimeter of a rectangle is equal to the sum of the four sides, or 2(length) + 2(width).

In the figure, *ABCD* is shown to have three right angles. Therefore, the fourth angle, at point *C*, is also a right angle, and *ABCD* is a rectangle.

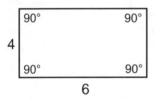

The area of a rectangle is equal to the length times the width.

From the figure,

$$A = 4 \times 6 = 24.$$

89. Parallelogram Properties

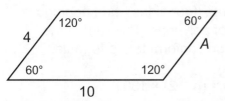

A parallelogram is a four-sided figure with two pairs of parallel sides. The opposite sides have equal length, and the angles opposite each other are equal. For example, "The figure shows a parallelogram. What is the length of side *A*?" Since the side opposite side *A* has length 4, therefore *A* = 4.

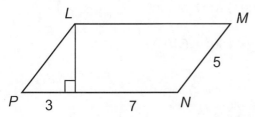

The area of a parallelogram is equal to the base times the height. For example, "What is the area of parallelogram *LMNP*?" First of all, the height of a parallelogram is not the same as the side of the parallelogram. The side *MN* = 5, and therefore the side *LP* = 5 also. Now we are ready to figure out the height, because we have two legs of a right triangle formed by a line from point *L* perpendicular to the base. Since we know one leg of the triangle is 3, and the hypotenuse is 5, then this is a 3-4-5 triangle. The height is 4, and the base is 7 + 3 = 10, so the area = base × height = 10 × 4 = 40.

90. Square Properties

A square is a rectangle that has four equal sides. The perimeter of a square is equal to four times the length of one side. The perimeter of square *RSTU* = 4 × 5 = 20. The area of a square is the length of one side squared. The area of square *RSTU* = 5^2 = 25.

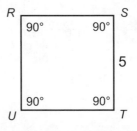

91. Polygon Properties

Triangles (three sides), squares (four sides), and pentagons (five sides) are all examples of polygons. The sum of the interior angles of every polygon conform to the formula:

$$\text{Sum of interior angles} = (n - 2) \times 180°$$

where n is the number of sides. Triangles, having three sides, work out to

$$(3 - 2) \times 180° = (1) \times 180° = 180°$$

Pentagons, having five sides, work out to

$$(5 - 2) \times 180° = (3) \times 180° = 540°$$

Circles

92. Circumference of a Circle

The circumference of a circle is given by the formula

$$\text{Circumference} = 2\pi r$$

For example, "What is the circumference of the circle in the figure?" Since the radius is 4,

$$\text{Circumference} = 2\pi(4) = 8\pi$$

93. Length of an Arc

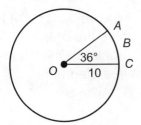

An arc is a portion of the circumference of a circle. The formula for the length of an arc uses n as the angle of the arc in degrees

$$\text{Length of an Arc} = \frac{n°}{360°} 2\pi r$$

For example, "What is the length of arc ABC?" The angle of the arc $n = 36°$, so

$$\text{Length of the Arc} = \frac{36°}{360°} 2\pi(10) = \frac{1}{10} 2\pi(10) = 2\pi$$

94. Area of a Circle

The area of a circle is given by the formula

$$A = \pi r^2$$

For example, "What is the area of the circle in the figure?" Since the radius of the circle is 7, then the area is

$$A = \pi(7^2) = 49\pi$$

95. Squares and Circles

The ACT testers like to have you figure out the value for a radius or a diameter before you are able to determine the area or perimeter they are asking you about in the problem. One common theme is to combine a circle and a square in a diagram.

For example, "What is the diameter of the circle in the figure?" Since the side of the square = 5, and all sides of a square are equal, then the radius = 5. The formula for the diameter is $D = 2r = 2(5) = 10$.

For another example, "What is the radius of the circle in the figure?" The square in this figure is on the outside of the circle. The side with length 5 is parallel to a diameter of the circle. Therefore, the diameter is $D = 5 = 2r$. The radius, which is what the question asked for, is $r = 5/2$.

And yet another example, "What is the diameter of the circle in the figure?" This time, the square is drawn inside the circle, and there is no diameter or radius of the circle to refer to. However, if we draw a diagonal of the square, it is also the base of a 45-45-90 triangle. Both legs of that triangle have length = 5, and therefore the hypotenuse is $5\sqrt{2}$. Therefore, $D = 5\sqrt{2}$.

96. Tangency

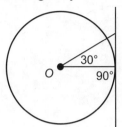

A line tangent to a circle is perpendicular from the radius of the line at that point. In other words, the radius and the tangent form a 90° angle. For example, "In the figure, the radius is 5, and a line tangent to the circle extends to meet another line that extends from the center of the circle, and forms a 30° angle with the original radius. What is the angle formed by the new line and the tangent?" Since the tangent is at a 90° angle from the radius, and the angle between the two lines extending from the center of the circle is 30°, this must be a 30-60-90 triangle. The unknown angle equals 60°.

Solids

97. Surface Area of a Rectangular Solid

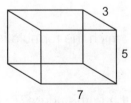

A rectangular solid has six faces, but each face is the same as its opposite face. For a rectangular solid with length $l = 7$, height $h = 5$, and width $w = 3$, the surface area is given as

Surface Area $= 2lw + 2wh + 2lh$

The surface area of the rectangular solid in the figure
$= 2(7)(3) + 2(3)(5) + 2(7)(5) = 42 + 30 + 70 = 142$.

NOTES:

98. Volume of a Rectangular Solid

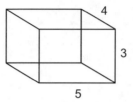

The volume of a rectangular solid is the length times the width times the height.

Volume of a Rectangular solid = *lwh*

For example, "What is the volume of the rectangular solid in the figure above?"

The volume = *lwh* = (5)(4)(3) = 60.

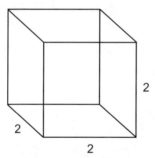

A special case is the volume of a cube, for which the formula is

Volume of a Cube = (side)^3

For example, "What is the volume of the cube in the figure?"

Volume = (side)^3 = (2)^3 = 8.

99. Volume of a Cylinder

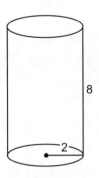

You can think of the volume of a cylinder as the area of the circle at the base times the height of the cylinder. The formula is

Volume of a Cylinder = $\pi r^2 h$

For example, "What is the volume of the cylinder in the figure?" The radius of the circle at the base is 2, and the height of the cylinder is 8.

$$V = \pi(2^2)(8) = 32\pi$$

NOTES:

Trigonometry

100. Sine, Cosine, and Tangent

In the triangle below, angle Θ gives the reference for the opposite side (side *a*) and the adjacent side (side *b*). The hypotenuse is side *c*. As far as the ACT is concerned, the trig functions sine, cosine, and tangent are ratios relating to the triangle in the figure.

$$\sin\Theta = \frac{\text{Opposite}}{\text{Hypotenuse}} = \frac{a}{c}$$

$$\cos\Theta = \frac{\text{Adjacent}}{\text{Hypotenuse}} = \frac{b}{c}$$

$$\tan\Theta = \frac{\text{Opposite}}{\text{Adjacent}} = \frac{a}{b}$$

The best memory trick to remember this is "SOH-CAH-TOA" which is pronounced like "Soak a toe, Ahh!"

CHAPTER 9

Reading

40 questions in 35 minutes! The ACT reading section is *not* a test of your ability to read slowly, carefully, and meticulously. Rather, the ACT reading section is going to require you to take a lesson in effective speed reading, because in 35 minutes you will have to read four passages—each about 800 words long—and answer 40 questions (yep, all in 35 minutes). Those lovely ACT creators are again relying on *Time Panic* to mess with your head. (We know - how rude!)

This means you'll have to have to find the precarious balance between "only read words that contain the letter v" (which would be no good…*very* bad idea) and "read like mankind's very existence hinges on your interpretation of this text" (which we hope would

NOTES:

force you into the most meticulous study session the world has ever known). Tiptoeing on either end of the spectrum would be disastrous on the ACT—but don't get too flustered. Turn a couple pages and check out the plethora of tips we've compiled to help you make the most of your time.

As promised, to save a few seconds on exam day, here are the …

Directions: *This test contains four passages, each followed by several questions. After reading a passage, select the best answer to each question and fill in the corresponding oval on your answer sheet. You are allowed to refer to the passage while answering the questions.*

memorize the **DIRECTIONS**

At the beginning of each passage will be a header containing the title, author, year, and any other information the writers find necessary for placing the piece into context.

PASSAGE TYPES

There are four different types of passages in the ACT reading section. These passages are vastly different in their writing styles, so we recommend that all students spend some time browsing literature beyond their typical library collection. To get an idea of what students should scope out, each type of passage featured on the ACT is described below.

Prose Fiction

These pieces are either "flash fiction" or excerpts from a short story or novel. The questions that accompany a fictional piece focus largely on the mood (emotions evoked by the prose) and the tone (the writer's attitude toward the subject). Additionally, questions regarding the characters' relationships with one another will arise.

Humanities

Literature from the Humanities section covers a wide range of subjects including (but not limited to) art, film, philosophy, and theater. Written about historical people and events, these pieces will contain important facts that may need to be regurgitated later (psst, what we're saying here is, "Get to underlining"). Like the previous section, however, you should also take note of the passage's mood and the author's tone.

Social Studies

Typically an objective presentation of research findings, the Social Studies passage discusses topics such as anthropology or psychology. For this passage's questions, you will want to pay close attention to inferences, main ideas, arguments, the relationship between causes and effects, and new vocabulary.

Natural Science

Heavy on scientific jargon, data, and figures, this section takes excerpts from scientific writing sources such as lab reports and textbooks and covers topics from anatomy to zoology. As you read, underline important data and *italicized* vocabulary and make note of important cause-effect relationships.

Test Prep Alert: While you may feel nervous about one or more of these topics, keep this in mind: there is no need for any knowledge of *any* given topic beyond the content of the passage. The point of the reading section is to test your ability to read wisely, not to recall information you already do or don't know. This means you should be able to pick up on mood and tone, recognize and make logical deductions and inferences, and analyze statistics and facts as they are presented. Ideally, having made it through twelve or thirteen years of the educational system has already made these skills second nature.

SCORING

You will receive three scores for this section: one will be from Natural Science and Social Studies, one will be from Prose Fiction and Humanities, and the last will be your composite score (calculated by averaging the two aforementioned scores).

TYPES OF QUESTIONS

Of the 40 questions you will be confidently and successfully answering (right?), 14 will be "referring questions." These questions literally have you refer to citations—no logic involved. The other 26 are the

NOTES:

"reasoning questions" which require you to make logical inferences, deductions, and conclusions based on the content of the prose. While this may seem like a stretch for a 35-minute time period, these questions don't necessitate much more than some common sense.

In case you still don't believe us, here is an ACT-friendly passage and a description and sample of each question type.

From **The Sea Wolf** by Jack London, 1904

The noises grew indistinct, though I heard a final and despairing chorus of screams in the distance, and knew that the Martinez had gone down. Later, - how much later I have no knowledge, - I came to myself with a start of fear. I was alone. I could hear no calls or cries - only the sound of the waves, made weirdly hollow and reverberant by the fog. A panic in a crowd, which partakes of a sort of community of interest, is not so terrible as a panic when one is by oneself; and such a panic I now suffered. Whither was I drifting? The red-faced man had said that the tide was ebbing through the Golden Gate. Was I, then, being carried out to sea? And

the life-preserver in which I floated? Was it not liable to go to pieces at any moment? I had heard of such things being made of paper and hollow rushes which quickly became saturated and lost all buoyancy. And I could not swim a stroke. And I was alone, floating, apparently, in the midst of a grey primordial vastness. I confess that a madness seized me, that I shrieked aloud as the women had shrieked, and beat the water with my numb hands.

How long this lasted I have no conception, for a blankness intervened, of which I remember no more than one remembers of troubled and painful sleep. When I aroused, it was as after centuries of time; and I saw, almost above me and emerging from the fog, the bow of a vessel, and three triangular sails, each shrewdly lapping the other and filled with wind. Where the bow cut the water there was a great foaming and gurgling, and I seemed directly in its path. I tried to cry out, but was too exhausted. The bow plunged down, just missing me and sending a swash of water clear over my head. Then the long, black side of the vessel began slipping past, so near that I could have touched it with my hands. I tried to reach it, in a mad resolve to claw into the wood with my nails, but my arms were heavy and lifeless. Again I strove to call out, but made no sound.

The stern of the vessel shot by, dropping, as it did so, into a hollow between the waves; and I caught a glimpse of a man standing at the wheel, and of another man who seemed to be doing little else than smoke a cigar. I saw the smoke issuing from his lips as he slowly turned his head and glanced out over the water in my direction. It was a careless, unpremeditated glance, one of those haphazard things men do when they have no immediate call to do anything in particular, but act because they are alive and must do something.

But life and death were in that glance. I could see the vessel being swallowed up in the fog; I saw the back of the man at the wheel, and the head of the other man turning, slowly turning, as his gaze struck the water and casually lifted along it toward me. His face wore an absent expression, as of deep thought, and I became afraid that if his eyes did light upon me he would nevertheless not see me. But his eyes did light upon me, and looked squarely into mine; and he did see me, for he sprang to the wheel, thrusting the other man aside, and whirled it round and round, hand over hand, at the same time shouting orders of some sort. The vessel seemed to go off at a tangent to its former course and leapt almost instantly from view into the fog.

NOTES:

I felt myself slipping into unconsciousness, and tried with all the power of my will to fight above the suffocating blankness darkness that was rising around me. A little later I heard the stroke of oars, growing nearer and nearer, and the calls of a man. When he was very near I heard him crying, in vexed fashion, "Why in hell don't you sing out?" This meant me, I thought, and then the blankness and darkness rose over me.

Now for ACT-style questions...

General Passage

Typically the first question(s) following a passage, these questions inquire about the purpose, tone, perspective and logical argument of the author as well as the relationships between different parts of the passage. Furthermore, these are the only questions you should ever consider answering without revisiting the text (though this is *not* to say you *shouldn't* revisit the text).

This passage is primarily

A)   a scientific description of old ships.
B)   a first-person story of getting saved at sea.
C)   a plea for better ocean safety.
D)   an opinion about good Samaritans.
E)   a general discussion on sailing vessels.

Answer: B

Compare and Contrast

These questions, frequently found in the Sciences and Social Studies passages, ask about the similarities and differences between two or more concepts, opinions, or facts. You will often be seeking the major difference or similarity between them.

In the second paragraph, our narrator writes, "for a blankness intervened." Choose the phrase that best matches its meaning.

A)   He forgot details of his story.

B)   He can't see clearly.

C)   He fell unconscious due to hypothermia.

D)   He doesn't know which way he's drifting.

E)   He got hit on the head when his own ship went down.

Answer: C

Specific Details

Questions of this sort refer to particular facts within the prose, thus requiring you to nab bits of information from the passage. Unfortunately, these questions test your ability to read *extremely carefully*, meaning the tidbits may be minute details. But don't forget that you can always seek out specific information once you know what you need, so don't let this kind of question bog you down (after all, this is why underlining is a helpful tool).

In the fourth paragraph, we are told that

A)   there are at least three men occupying the ship.

B)   two men are chatting at the wheel of the ship.

C)   two men aboard the ship simultaneously spot the narrator.

D)   it was not the man at the wheel who noticed the narrator.

E)   neither of the men take notice of the drifter.

Answer: D

Cause and Effect

Some questions will test your ability to recognize causality or to make predictions based on a presented pattern of cause and effect. Sometimes this means determining which of two related events caused the other; sometimes this means making a forecast for a character's response to an event that he or she has not previously encountered. Both situations require the ability to recognize a causal sequence.

If the narrator had not been seen by the men in the boat, it is likely that he would have

A)   lost hope in rescue and silently watched the ship drift away.
B)   began waving his arms in the air.
C)   let go of the life-preserver and swam toward the bow of the ship.
D)   grabbed onto the ship and tried to climb up.
E)   shrieked out for help.

Answer: A

Unsupported Statements

Some of the most common questions asked on the ACT reading section, these questions present four statements and ask you to find the one which is unsupported by the passage. The most efficient way to answer these questions is to go through each statement and find its support (or lack thereof) in the passage. If the statement is supported in the passage, cross it out; if there's no evidence of the statement in the passage, you just might have found your answer. However, be sure to check *all* statements before choosing, as one seemingly unsupported statement may just be an induction that you had not yet considered.

Despite our narrator struggling with drowning and hypothermia, he still manages to

A)   learn the name of his rescuing vessel.

B)   make observations about his own panic.

C)   grab onto the rescue vessel.

D)   save others from the Martinez.

E)   call out for help.

Answer: B

To consider the other question types you'll be seeing on the ACT, read on to the next passage.

NOTES:

---

*From **The Fat and the Thin** by Emile Zola, 1873*

When Florent was brought before an investigating magistrate, without anyone to defend him, and without any evidence being adduced, he was accused of belonging to a secret society; and when he swore that this was untrue, the magistrate produced the scrap of paper from amongst the documents before him: "Taken with blood-stained hands. Very dangerous." That was quite sufficient. He was condemned to transportation. Six weeks afterwards, one January night, a gaoler awoke him and locked him up in a courtyard with more than four hundred other prisoners. An hour later this first detachment started for the pontoons and exile, handcuffed and guarded by a double file of gendarmes with loaded muskets. They crossed the Austerlitz bridge, followed the line of the boulevards, and so reached the terminus of the Western Railway line. It was a joyous carnival night. The windows of the restaurants on the boulevards glittered with lights. At the top of the Rue Vivienne, just at the spot where he ever saw the young woman lying dead--that unknown young woman whose image he always bore with him--he now beheld a large carriage in which a party of masked women, with bare shoulders and laughing voices, were venting their impatience at being detained, and expressing their horror of that endless procession of convicts. The whole of the way from Paris to Havre the prisoners never received a mouthful of bread or a drink of water. The officials had forgotten to give them their rations before starting, and it was not till thirty-six hours afterwards, when they had been stowed away in the hold of the frigate Canada, that they at last broke their fast.

No, Florent had never again been free from hunger. He recalled all the past to mind, but could not recollect a single hour of satiety. He had become dry and withered; his stomach seemed to have shrunk; his skin clung to his bones. And now that he was back in Paris once more, he found it fat and sleek and flourishing, teeming with food in the midst of the darkness. He had returned to it on a couch of vegetables; he lingered in its midst encompassed by unknown masses of food which still and ever increased and disquieted him. Had that happy carnival night continued throughout those seven years, then? Once again he saw the glittering windows on the boulevards, the laughing women, the luxurious, greedy city which he had quitted on that far-away January night; and it seemed to him that everything had expanded and increased in harmony with those huge markets, whose gigantic breathing, still heavy from the indigestion of the previous day, he now began to hear.

Old Mother Chantemesse had by this time made up her mind to buy a dozen bunches of turnips. She put them in her apron, which she held closely pressed to her person, thus making herself look yet more corpulent than she was; and for some time longer she lingered there, still gossiping in a drawling voice. When at last she went away, Madame Francois again sat down by the side of Florent.

"Poor old Mother Chantemesse!" she said; "she must be at least seventy-two. I can remember her buying turnips of my father when I was a mere chit. And she hasn't a relation in the world; no one but a young hussy whom she picked up I don't know where and who does nothing but bring her trouble. Still, she manages to live, selling things by the ha'p'orth and clearing her couple of francs profit a day. For my own part, I'm sure that I could never spend my days on the foot- pavement in this horrid Paris! And she hasn't even any relations here!"

"You have some relations in Paris, I suppose?" she asked presently, seeing that Florent seemed disinclined to talk.

Florent did not appear to hear her. A feeling of distrust came back to him. His head was teeming with old stories of the police, stories of spies prowling about at every street corner, and of women selling the secrets which they managed to worm out of the unhappy fellows they deluded. Madame Francois was sitting close beside him and certainly looked perfectly straightforward and honest, with her big calm face, above which was bound a black and yellow handkerchief. She seemed about five and thirty years of age, and was somewhat stoutly built, with a certain hardy beauty due to her life in the fresh air. A pair of black eyes, which beamed with kindly tenderness, softened the more masculine characteristics of her person. She certainly was inquisitive, but her curiosity was probably well meant.

This passage will help us examine the other question types.

What He Said

Much like the exact opposite of questions in the "Unsupported Statements" category, these questions ask you to seek direct citations in the text and, based on their context, answer questions about them. Sometimes a line number will be provided. Other times you will need to seek similar words and/or phrases (e.g. "The ship's figurehead held the form of a mythical monster from the depths of the Bermuda Triangle's cursed seas," being paraphrased as, "The ship's design arose from a mythological sea-dwelling beast in the Bermuda Triangle."). If the latter is the case, choose a few key terms and search for them grouped together. In either case, once you've found the referenced line(s), read a sentence or two before and after the citation in question and then refer to your options.

Judging from the passage, the story takes place

A)   in post-Revolution Paris, around 1800.
B)   in Canada, 1920.
C)   in Germany during WWII.
D)   in a Civil War concentration camp.
E)   None of the above

Answer: A

Rhetorical Analysis

Questions of this sort require students to take in a paragraph or single sentence and, based on context, determine its function in the whole. These questions may also refer to a portion of a sentence that uses figurative language; for these, a student must be able to translate the creative image into a literal statement. Whether the question refers to a plain-Jane sentence or to an artistic use of figurative language, the student must have a general understanding of the message to be able to place the excerpt into context and explain its purpose.

Based on the first three sentences of the passage, we know that

A)   the counter revolution was conducted fairly.
B)   food merchants are dirty creatures.
C)   Parisian aristocracy is calmly intelligent.
D)   there were rushed show trials in Paris.
E)   radicals needed to be transported by force.

Answer: D

Vocabulary

Questions pertaining to vocabulary are designed to test your ability to deduce the meaning of a word based on the context in which it was used. A line number is generally provided for the word in question, so all you need to do is determine which option is the closest synonym.

According to the opening paragraph, the word transportation means

A)   horse and buggy.

B)   punishment and forced exile.

C)   steam train.

D)   cab fare.

E)   None of the above

Answer: B

EFFECTIVE, SPEEDY READING

If we're going to prompt you to *not* read as if you're trying to understand whatever it is that William Blake is talking about, we should probably tell you how you *should* read, no?

NOTES:

The Keys to Underlining

Here are some of the cues writers generally use to say to the reader, "Hey, this bit is important!" When you find these cues during your scan, carefully read what follows—you're likely to need this information to answer the upcoming questions.

Underline or circle these as you encounter them in your reading!

Key Argument Presentation	Compare/Contrast	Examples
As	Although	As an illustration
Because (of)	And yet	Especially
Due to	At the same time	For example
For (the reason)	But	For instance
Since	In comparison	Including
	In contrast	In particular
Purpose	In the same manner	Namely
For fear that	However	Notably
In the hope that	Likewise	Particularly
In order to	Meanwhile	Specifically
So (that)	Nevertheless	To demonstrate
With this in mind	Nonetheless	To illustrate
	Notwithstanding	**Reasoning**
	On the contrary	Because
Cause and Effect	On the other hand	Due to the fact
As a result	Similarly	Is based on
Because of this	While this is true	Is proved by
Due to	When in fact	Is shown by
For this reason	Whereas	Which follows from
Consequently		Is a consequence of
So (that)		Since
Therefore		For
Thus	**Counterexamples**	
	Admittedly	**Conclusion**
	Even so	Accordingly
Elaboration on Idea	Even though	As a result
Additionally	Despite	Consequently
Also	Indeed	Hence
Besides	Nevertheless	In brief
Equally important	Notwithstanding	In conclusion
Further(more)	Regardless	In short
Incidentally		In summary
Moreover		On the whole
		Therefore
		Thus
		To conclude

Skim the Surface

Give the passage a once-over; seek the aforementioned cues, underline important information, and get an overall feeling for the theme, mood, and tone. You should also take a mental note of the format of the passage, as you may wish to return to one section during your double-take (this is not recommended for the fiction prose, though, as it is unlikely to have a predictable/navigable format).

As you read, avoid falling victim to your desire to master the passage—especially on your first pass. This may be very hard for some of you brainiac alpha nerds out there, so you might want to practice light skimming. Consider this: you can always refer back to a passage, but you cannot undo ten minutes wasted on memorizing an entire prose.

Wait, What Are They Asking?

Avoiding the answer options, *carefully* read the questions. We repeat: *Do not read the answer options prior to formulating your own response, as the options may influence your thinking in a very sneaky, wrong way* (those ACT writers are just ruthless!).

NOTES:

Double-Take

Return to the text and seek proof for your answer. Remember, all correct responses will be either explicitly stated or inferred in the passage. If you don't find it, *it's not correct*. If this is the case, make a quick guess, mark the question for revisiting, and continue onto the page's other questions.

Round Two

Once the rest of the page is complete, return to any unanswered questions. If you now know the answer (from all that re-reading and contemplating), congrats! If not, eliminate bad answers to increase your chance of guessing correctly. Guessing from all four gives you a 25% chance of getting it right, guessing from three gives you 33%, and guessing from only two gives you a 50% chance—so knock out those bad answers and guess with confidence.

ADDITIONAL READING TIPS:

 Do not try to become an expert on the passages found in the reading section, especially not on the Science passage. Instead of becoming weighed down by details, take a step back and check out the big picture.

Pay extra attention to the first and last paragraph as well as the first and last sentence of each paragraph. Writers tend to work in a form of "argument, proof and examples, argument." And, as stated earlier, the argument (or objective) is the most important piece of the prose.

NOTES:

 An active pencil is an active mind. To fend off the sleeps, underline important information—but before you get carried away, know that it's best to avoid over-marking your booklet in this section. Your time is better spent reading questions carefully, paying close attention to the author's objective, and referring to information which you've underlined—*not* rewriting the author's ideas and hence reading your own opinion. Information you should consider underlining:

1. The main idea
2. Logic reversal vocabulary (but, yet, in spite of, unless, while, except, far from, rather, even though, despite)
3. Names and places
4. Words relating to sequence (including cause and effect)
5. Words relating to character relationships

NOTES:

 Know your reading speed *long* before test day. This will help you estimate a realistic time limit per question and thereby help you detour around speed-bumps Remember: those super difficult questions aren't worth a *fraction* more than the easy, peasy guys.

 Adjust your speed as you read. Carefully analyze the author's objective and perspective in the prose. When it comes to supporting ideas and examples, however, limit yourself to a less time-consuming scan.

 Questions should be read with more diligence than the passage itself. You're more likely to incorrectly interpret a question than misread the passage. And since your score is based on the questions you answer, your lasting impression of the prose is of negligible importance.

 Any answer you choose should be explicitly supported by the prose. The correct answer to questions in the reading section will not require you to make any complex logical deductions. Do not seek "hidden" or "alternate" meanings—this isn't an advanced literature analysis class!

NOTES:

 When you run into answer options which contain absolute language (e.g. no, none, never, all, always, every, etc.), be extremely wary. This diction often identifies wrong answers.

 Formulate a response prior to looking at your options. Answers are written to be "approximately correct," meaning you could easily opt for an incorrect answer because your thinking was swayed by the oh-so-close option.

 Always refer back to the passage prior to answering questions. Aside from very general questions regarding tone, theme, or overall message, this technique will ensure you are answering based on the passage and not your own perspective.

 For general passage questions (e.g. "What is the author's purpose in writing this piece?"), if the answer is not immediately clear, circle it and move on to the other questions that require you to revisit the passage. During these revisits, the idea may become obvious and negate your need to re-read the passage to comprehend the purpose, tone, et cetera.

NOTES:

 If you feel uncomfortably rushed when trying to read and answer the questions for all four passages of sample reading tests (as many students do), dedicate your time to carefully covering the three types of passages you find most pleasant and comprehensible. Once you've finished these three, do what you can to make educated guesses on the fourth. It's better to do extremely well on three passages and guess on the fourth than to sloppily cover all four. Consider this:

1. Many students read too fast to cover all four passages. Reading all four allots a meager 8.75 minutes per passage. Consequently, students only have an average of 6 correct answers per passage. This gives them an average Reading score of 21.

2. Students who choose to pay close attention to only three passages for 11 minutes each tend to get 8 to 10 questions correct. The last two minutes can then be spent guessing on the last passage which, statistically, gives them another 2 to 3 points. This method can yield a score of 26 – 33 (much better than 21!).

If you're facing a serious time crunch, look for questions that indicate a line reference. These questions will be easier to complete since you won't be tasked with a keyword search.

Of all the advice we can give to you, we'd like to wrap up this chapter by reinforcing this super duper helpful tip: *read more*. And challenge yourself! Read medical journals and enjoy a classic short story by Washington Irving; browse financial magazines and check out that anthropology article on Ardi, the *Ardipithecus ramidus*; analyze Ayn Rand's *The Cult of Moral Grayness* and dissect a few page's of Freud's *The Ego and the Id*.

Whatever you do, don't stick to one genre. Read all or part of *MANY* things, and absorb and incorporate each writing style into your knowledge base. And when you've finished each piece of literature, delight a parent or a pal with your discoveries: summarize for them what you've read and share your thoughts. Annoy your friends with esoteric tidbits you pick up here and there. Verbalizing this information will test whether or not you've truly comprehended the information. If you can't do this, perhaps it's a sign that you need to do more reading from that particular piece's genre. And for goodness

NOTES:

sake, read each and every piece enthusiastically. Even if you don't *really* delight in the techniques used to hasten the drying of latex house paint, pretend you do—you'll be able to recall the information easier if you trick your brain into thinking that it just *loves* paint. Go on: show that paint some love!

CHAPTER 10
Science

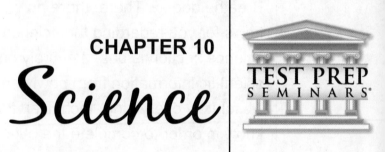

TEST PREP
SEMINARS

Breathe deeply. There, there now…we have good news for you regarding the science section: the science section is based entirely on your ability to pull scientific information from newly presented information. Absolutely everything "technical" that you need to know in order to complete the questions will be within the problem itself. So, *again*, don't fret that you aren't into botany! Just make sure you have some basic information-extraction skills (which we're here to coach you on) and you'll do just fine.

In 35 minutes, a total of 40 questions must be answered on seven passages. Unfortunately, this section tends to be the hardest to study for because, ironically, it's actually not very scientific. But of all five sections, science persistently dupes test takers, thus producing the lowest test average (yep, even worse than math, and even among those smarties who score in the 30s).

The silly thing about all this is that it's not even that difficult…honestly. While the graphical representations of data and the written passages often appear elaborate and complex, the questions themselves are actually quite easy. If you can get past the daunting presentation of the science section, it'll be smooth sailing.

Before we begin our discussion, let's take a look at the …

> **Directions:** *Each of the following seven passages is followed by several questions. After reading each passage, decide on the best answer and fill in the corresponding oval on your answer sheet. You are allowed to refer to the passage while answering the questions. Calculator use is not allowed on this test.*

memorize the **DIRECTIONS**

(Don't freak over the last sentence. You won't need a calculator.)

The seven aforementioned passages are broken up into three data representation sections with 5 questions each, three research summaries with 6 questions each, and one passage on conflicting viewpoints with 7 questions.

POSSIBLE PASSAGE SUBJECTS

While it's true that we could give you a detailed list of topics from which the ACT writers pull, we're not going to waste the ink. The list is enormous and, quite frankly, useless. Expecting someone to prepare for the science section by studying microbiology, meteorology, electrochemistry, thermodynamics, physics, anatomy, physiology, psychology—O.K., O.K., you get the point: it's just way too much! And expecting someone to prepare for all of that is insane; it would be like training to swim at the summer Olympics when all you really need to do is cross an inch-deep, mile-wide puddle. So instead of turning your mind into goo, we'll help you prepare by telling you what to expect and which general skills you should exercise.

PASSAGE TYPES

1. Conflicting Viewpoints

This essay of sorts will present two or more theories in which the scientists are singing in perfect harmony, bickering over the details, or going through a nasty divorce. As the drama unfolds, contemplate the "Big Picture" and <u>underline</u> key difference and similarities between the theories. Avoiding a jargon jam is pertinent to these passages; knowing that some Latin word has a different effect at temperature x than y is much more important than knowing that the weird word means "an organelle which prepares proteins to be transported out of a cell." For these passages, your task will simply be to discuss where these viewpoints agree and where they disagree.

2. **Charts & Graphs**

These passages discuss the content of a chart, graph, illustration, or table. While the introduction to these passages puts the forthcoming data into context, the introduction is of significantly lower importance and should thus be allotted very little time. Focus, instead, on the chart, diagram, table, etc. Questions following the data will test your ability to comprehend and utilize the represented information—and sometimes you can do this without any reading whatsoever.

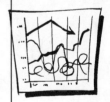

3. **Experiments**

Containing content akin to that of Data Representation, these passages are similar to scientific journals: they generally present the goals, methodology, and findings of two or more related experiments. These summaries should be read with more diligence than the text of data representation and of chart and graph passages. Additionally, since there will likely be fewer visual indicators in this section, jotting down key words is particularly helpful when you need to find information to answer the forthcoming questions. These accompanying questions are a mixture of those seen in Conflicting Viewpoints passages and Data Representation passages.

THE SCIENTIFIC THOUGHT PROCESS

There are two thought processes that you will run into during your brush with the ACT's science section and you will thus need to differentiate between the two: *application* and *experimentation*. The test generally dedicates more time to experimentation, but it also asks test takers to perform application, so knowing a bit about both will help you in the long run.

Application: General Rule → Specific Fact

When scientists go from a general rule to a specific fact, they are taking what they already know about a system and applying it to a unique scenario. These types of processes show that, since Y is part of system A, it can be said that the attributes of Y are those of A or that Z follows a predictable pattern based on what we know about B. Below is an example of application.

> A robotic drone was built with a 3.5 gallon container. If water is known to weigh 8.3 pounds per gallon when stored at 70° Fahrenheit, how many pounds of water will the drone be able to transport at any one time at 70° Fahrenheit?

Tips

The specific fact can be found by filling and weighing the 3.5 gallon container, or it can be calculated as so:

3.5 gal × 8.3 pounds/gal = 29.05 pounds.

Experimentation: Specific Fact → General Rule

When scientists form and test a *hypothesis* (also known as a theory) they are creating a *hypothesis* to describe a system as a whole based on their observation(s) of something more specific. In such cases, the experiment is designed to assign universality to a perceived trend. While a hypothesis of universality cannot always be tested *in every possible scenario,* it is possible for a hypothesis to be so well-documented that it is considered law of nature (gravity, for one, is in this category). Below is an example of hypothesis formation and testing.

For three consecutive years, the month of October has been filled with reports of rampaging elephants in the South Asian city of Prjapatibasti. With authorities fearing similar behavior from the zoo's elephants (which were recently obtained from this same area), an animal behaviorist investigated the potential cause of the elephant's oddly destructive outbursts: gluttonous consumption of rice beer.

To test the behaviorist's hypothesis that the alcohol consumption was the cause of the feared behavior, a team constructs a "safe zone" in which a few of the elephants are given small amounts of alcohol and monitored for safety reasons as well as for behavioral changes. Sure enough, the buzzed beasts progressed from stumbling into one another to slapping belligerently at the padded walls. After documenting the behavior well enough to form a general rule of correlation, the tipsy elephants were kept clear of any and all alcohol.

(See, science can be fun. And if you're wondering, Prjapatibasti *is* a real place and its elephants *really do* get inebriated and cause a ruckus.)

NOTES:

Science

ASPECTS OF EXPERIMENTATION

You will need to be savvy to the scientific method in order to successfully answer questions following an experiment passage. Familiarize yourself with the following terminology.

Variables are the aspects of an experiment which undergo some sort of change. Those aspects which are purposefully altered by scientists are called the _independent variables_ and those aspects which are affected by the alteration are called the _dependent variables_. The group containing the manipulated dependent variables is called the _experimental group_. In addition to the experimental group is the _control group_ in which all factors are kept in the same condition as those in the experimental group, minus the independent variables. By providing a baseline to which the experimental group will be compared, the control group is used to identify the effect of the variation in the independent variable.

To demonstrate, consider an experiment which analyzes the effects of flash photography on the longevity of artwork.

A frame was built to simultaneously paint sixteen canvases. Each canvas was of similar constitution and received a uniform amount of paint from a shared source. A unit was also designed to isolate the paintings from one another and provide each with an electronic flash unit and an equal amount of natural light. Every other painting received zero flashes per day, whereas the other eight were assigned a value of one through eight flashes per day. After three months, a blind study was performed: conservators from a local museum, without being informed of the research, each analyzed the samples for deterioration.

Those paintings which received no flashes are considered the *control group* and those which were exposed to flash(es) are part of the *experimental group*. The *independent variable* is the number of flashes each painting received and the *dependent variable* is the amount of deterioration caused by the light and heat.

Not too hard, is it?

READING A SCIENTIFIC PASSAGE

Scientific articles and research summaries are notoriously difficult to read, and for the simple reason that jargon can be downright perplexing. If you wish to do well on the science section, it is intrinsically important that you be able to look beyond the truckload of technical terminology that will be dumped on you. After all, the greatest time trap in this section is simply getting through the reading itself. If you're unable to accept that there will surely be words beyond your vocabulary, and that during the ACT isn't the time to expand your vocabulary, how in the world do you suppose you'll be able to read seven passages and correctly answer all, if any, of the forty questions *when you only have 35 minutes*? (Here's a hint: you won't.)

Since the tongue of the scientific community is vast and (sometimes) rather alien, the answer to this jargon jam is to either *get over it* and ignore the exotic language, or to normalize that sinking feeling via repeated exposure to scientific articles and research summaries.

Once you feel confident in your ability to snub the shoptalk, the passages are best handled in the following manner:

1. Carefully read the introduction. These few lines will help orient your thinking and assist in developing a plan of attack (that is, develop a list of keywords to seek). Consider the following example introduction.

> *A suspected <u>decrease in firefly population</u> prompted local wildlife conservators to study the <u>effects of light pollution</u> on the <u>mating habits</u> of beetles of the Coleoptera order. The experiment placed local specimens in synthetic environments in which researchers tightly controlled and <u>varied the amount of light</u> given to each group. Researchers measured the effects of light pollution by counting the <u>number of larvae</u> produced in a <u>two month</u> span by the specimens.*

The words we've <u>underlined</u> are those we consider to be important keywords. These <u>underlined</u> words will be the backbone of the data you must extract from the passage, so pencil-in a visual marker for any information which includes these keywords.

2. Skim the entire article. Avoid trying to gain a comprehensive understanding of the content; to do so would require a background in the subject or entirely too much time to analyze the text. As you skim, underline those key words and make a mental road map of the passage.

3. Check out the question. Without jumping ahead to the possible answers, *very carefully* read the question stem. Make sure you know exactly what is being asked of you and consider the information you will be seeking.

4. Revisit the passage. Skim your notes and review your mental road map for any data relevant to the question stem. Upon locating the desired information, read a sentence (or two) to put what you're reading into context. **Beware** of words such as *increase, decrease, except, and not.*

5. Match your answer to one of the options. Granted, the correct response may sound a little like gibberish to you, but if your answer alludes to the same idea as one of the options (though in a much more straightforward manner, of course), go with your instincts and circle your choice.

CHARTS & GRAPHS

There are four levels of chart and graph comprehension tested on the ACT: the ability to identify information, to translate information from graphical to written form (and vice versa), to utilize data to infer unstated information, and to identify the trends which help forecast future steps in an experiment. To accomplish these tasks, it is important to recognize the following:

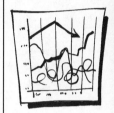

- **What is being represented on the X- & Y-axis or in the columns and rows**

- **Units of Measurement**

- **Whether scales are continuous (generally in numerical intervals) or categorical (data clustered into discernible groups)**

- **Maximums and Minimums**

- **Trends**

- **Critical Points**

- **Proportionality**

Below are examples of the sorts of charts and graphs that you will encounter on the ACT. For each data representation, try to identify the aforementioned items prior to reading the given descriptions.

Example 1

This example is the data collected from a quantitative analysis performed via High-Performance Liquid Chromatography (HPLC). HPLC uses the unique properties of molecules to separate, identify, and measure the components of a liquid mixture.

High-Performance Liquid
Chromatography Readout

Concentration of Caffeine (ppm)	Area
24.7	2889359
37.4	4321095
62.4	7161988
125	14243783

- **Columns and Rows.** There are two columns (vertical groups): "Concentration of Caffeine" and "Area". The unlabeled rows (horizontal groups) are understood to be individual trials.

- **Units of Measurement.** Depending on which column you're looking at, the unit of measurement changes: concentration is in parts per million (ppm) and area is unlabeled to indicate that it is in constant, arbitrary units.

- **Continuous or Categorical.** Once again, the values listed do not indicate that they represent a group of values or measurements, so our scale is continuous (i.e. each value represents a single trial/reading).

- **Maximum and Minimum Values.** The readout of interest (or the dependent variable) is generally found in the second column (or row if the chart is grouped horizontally); hence, the area has a maximum value when at a concentration of 125 ppm and has a minimum value when at a concentration of 24.7 ppm.

- **Trends.** As the concentration of caffeine is increased, the area increases.

- **Critical Points.** The chart follows a linear trend, and there don't appear to be any abnormal responses, so there aren't any critical points.

- **Proportionality.** The concentration and the area are directly proportional: as ppm increases, area increases.

Example 2

The melting and boiling points of water change with atmospheric pressure. Below is a graphical representation of this trend and a description of its important aspects (which, of course, you won't be reading until you've tried to identify them yourself...).

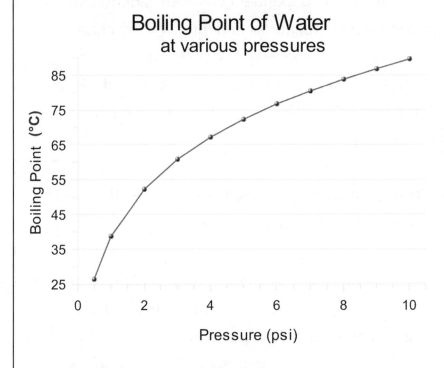

Boiling Point of Water
at various pressures

- **X- & Y-Axis.** Pressure is reported along the x-axis and the boiling point is reported along the y-axis.

- **Units of Measurement.** Pressure is described in pounds per square inch (psi) and the boiling point is described in degrees Celsius.

- **Continuous or Categorical.** Both the x- and y-axes are expressed as continuous scales, as each point represents a single reading.

- **Maximum and Minimum Values.** Treating this information as finite (i.e. the data does not extend below 0.5 psi or above 10 psi), the minimum boiling point is approximately 26°C and the maximum boiling point is approximately 90°C.

- **Trends.** As pressure increases, the boiling point of water appears to increase.

- **Critical Points.** There are no sharp critical points here, but we can say that from 0.5 to 1.0 psi exists the largest increase in boiling point (based on the sharp slope between the two points).

- **Proportionality.** The boiling point is proportional to pressure.

Example 3

Getting bored? Hang in there. This is the last one.

After marketing agents at BreakYourBank, Inc. (BYB, Inc.), noticed a sharp decline in sales at Mulberry Mall, an analysis of the shopping center's customer base was performed. The graph below represents the study's findings:

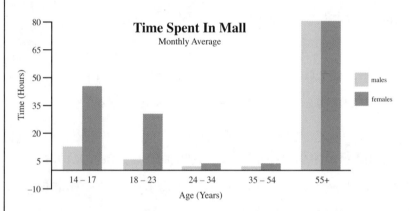

Unfortunately for BYB, Inc., the analysis provided a few conclusions.

- Early teens, who were assumed to be the largest source of income to Mulberry Mall, spend the second-to-most time at the mall. Unfortunately, they also spend the second-to-least money.

- The elders (generally gathered in flocks of flashy wind suits) are spotted nearly twice as often as early teens, but only spend a net average of $0.21 per hour passed power walking.

- The group that provides the most concentrated source of income per hour is males aged 24 - 34. Unfortunately, this income is often temporary, as the most substantial purchase made by this group (an engagement ring), is returned within the 30 day refund window.

Following this examination, BYB, Inc. reconsidered the mall's motto: "We can make your wallet lighter!" Needless to say, it was a bit too late.

- **X- & Y-Axis.** The x-axis denotes different age groups and the y-axis indicates time.

- **Units of Measurement.** Age is reported in years and time is reported in hours.

- **Continuous or Categorical.** The y-axis is a continuous scale, but each measurement along the x-axis is broken up into two separate categories: males and females. See the difference between the first two examples and this one? *Continuous scales* have one measurement per point, but *categorical scales* have many measurements represented by a single point (i.e. an average of time spent in the mall by a random sampling of men aged 35–54.)

NOTES:

- **Maximum and Minimum Values.** Along the x axis, there is no maximum age (55+) but there is a minimum age of 14. Along the y-axis, males aged 24-34 are recorded as spending the minimum of one hour per month in the mall and males and females 55+ each spend the maximum average of 85 hours in the mall per month (presumably spent power walking and, occasionally, purchasing new shoelaces).

- **Trends.** Unfortunately for BreakYourBank, Inc., there only seem to be two trends:
  1. In general, females are a larger portion of the customer base. (Well that's not bad.)
  2. No one really seems to buy anything. (Eeek!)

- **Critical Points.** No critical points are evident on this graph; however, we predict that the stock prices of BYOB, Inc., will make a sharp dive circa … now.

- **Proportionality.** Considering only the data on the graph, there does not appear to be any sense of proportionality in this data.

So, you were able to pull all of the important information from the charts and graphs by identifying the 7 characteristics, right? That's a heck of a start! Keep reading—more help is on the way!

THE POWER OF GUESSTIMATION

Before you start making faces at us for deeming guessing to be a powerful tool on the ACT, be honest with yourself: if you meticulously dealt with each and every problem, you'd only be half-way done when time was called. Therefore, we call upon the magical powers of guesstimation!

If your science teacher never conjured this one up, guesstimation is the love-child of a guess and an estimation. Essentially, the idea is for you to make an educated guess at an approximate answer, thereby putting you in the ballpark of the actual answer.

Guesstimation is an awesome tool to use in lieu of carrying out calculations. Consider this example question:

> The velocity of an object is represented as a ratio between distance traveled and time traveled. If a projectile travels 22.5 meters in 5 seconds, what is its velocity?
>
> A. 4.0 m/s
> B. 4.5 m/s
> C. 5.0 m/s
> D. 5.5 m/s

You can either perform long division, or you can wield your guesstimation prowess. While the stubborn kids go for long division, let's get to guesstimating:

> We know that $20 \div 5 = 4$ and $25 \div 5 = 5$, so our answer must lie between 4 and 5. Well, look at that—there's only one! By guesstimation, we know our answer must be B, 4.5 m/s.

This method can also be applied in instances where it appears that extremely technical question are being asked. In these cases, take what you know (the education bit!) and make an estimate. Ladies and gentlemen, we have a guesstimation.

During the summer of 2006, scientists studied the appropriately named trap-jaw ant. This species of ant is famous for its powerful mandibles, which have been recorded as snapping its mouth closed at an astounding 145 miles per hour. The powerful jaws are not only useful for nabbing food, but also for snapping at the ground to propel the ant an amazing 3.2 inches into the air. To perform this feat, the ant must overcome gravity to an astonishing 100,000 G's (folks, that's more than 33,000 times the G's that any astronaut has ever experienced—and they go into space). If another ant were discovered to accelerate a little over 110,000 G's while performing this same maneuver, what is a reasonable estimate for the mandibles' closing speed?

NOTES:

A. 100 mph

B. 120 mph

C. 140 mph

D. 160 mph

You could easily construct a ratio of speed to G's, or you could recognize that overcoming gravity *more* necessitates a faster closing speed. And since we're relating speed to G-force, and the only speed above the trap-jaw ant's 145 mph is D, 160 mph, we can say "I guesstimate that an ant that produces 110,000 G's with

its terrifying jaw would also be able to snap its mouth shut at 160 mph." And you could say it with confidence. As you're now willing to admit, something that sounds as silly as "guesstimation" can be equally as powerful as your $200 graphing calculator. (Don't be upset; that supercomputer of yours will come in handy *some* day.)

ADDITIONAL SCIENCE TIPS

☺ Never try to fully comprehend the massive amount of information this section will throw at you. Your goal during the ACT is not to become a well-rounded intellect; rather, your goal is to correctly answer as many questions as possible. Only take away a general comprehension of the material and a mental road map of the details to be accessed later.

☺ Pay attention to *italicized* words. These terms will generally be followed by a definition, which may or may not arise in the question section. To make these stand out more than they already do, go ahead and <u>underline</u> them.

☺ Remain diligent by keeping your pencil active. Circle units of measurement and key/reversal words such as *decrease, increase, except,* and *not.*

Tips

☺ If you're having difficulty comprehending the material, break down the passage into a few key components. Ask yourself the following comprehension questions:

Tips

- What is the purpose of the experiment?
- What is being tested and why?
- What are the variables and the constants?
- How is the outcome affected by each variable change?

☺ Establish a form of shorthand in order to quickly take notes in the margins (e.g., Δ for change and $\propto$ for proportionality). Your notes should be written on the same line as their source so that super-brief notes such as "density" or "velocity Δ" can be quickly put into context without the need to frantically scan the original text.

☺ The first questions you are asked will be those which test your general understanding of the passage. *Do not skip these.* If you cannot answer this sort of question, you did not comprehend the passage well enough. Questions to follow will be more complex and rely heavily on your ability to relate details to the big picture.

NOTES:

☺ Make sure to choose an option which actually answers the question. Test writers often include answers which merely state something true about the passage without addressing the inquiry. Don't be tricked by this maneuver.

☺ If a question feels daunting, dispel all of that negative energy flooding in and toss out the jargon along with it. Mentally translate confusing questions into your own everyday language and, prior to viewing the multiple-choice answers, refer back to the passage. If you're still stumped, make a quick guess and move on.

☺ For questions in the science section that are heavy on visuals, skim the question(s) prior to reading the passage—the reading may be entirely superfluous and function only as a time-trap. (Note: For questions that require a reading, this technique will not set you back as you will know what to be looking for when you get around to the reading.)

☺ As you read through your answer options, cross out those which contradict the passage or draw on the tendency to extrapolate data (meaning, make a hasty generalization of the data and assume information beyond what is given to you).

Tips

☺ Never—we repeat, *never*—select any answer that isn't explicitly stated in the reading.

☺ The ACT does not construct scenarios in which an experiment is deliberately flawed. Therefore, when you come across a question as to whether or not a researcher made a mistake, or if the experiment methodology could be improved, don't give too much thought to the two "YES" options. You're better off checking out the reasons coupled with the two "NO" options. If you feel that there truly was a mistake made in the experiment, ask yourself: "Would I wager my USB-pet rock on this?" If you're willing to put your dear Googley-Eye on the line, maybe you should abandon this tip.

☺ Complete the science reading passages last. These passages are light on visual markers and are near impossible to answer with a quick data assessment (such as those in the data representation section). Try to only spend 60 to 90 seconds reading, labeling, and taking notes on each passage.

☺ If you find yourself at the five-minute mark with an unread passage, forgo trying to cram the literature in prior to addressing the question stems. Rather, look for questions of the data interpretation sort, as these can be quickly answered simply by viewing data from a table, graph, etc.

Tips

Tips

We can't be sure exactly what it is that keeps snagging students in this section. Even when they have inside-information on the ACT writers' trick of using big, scary words, many promising students *still* fall short of their full capacity. Is it because this is the last multiple-choice section, thus filling students' pants with pesky trap-jaw ants? Is it because the Reading section thoroughly exhausted their mental faculties since the last break? Or is it because they ignored what we said about avoiding coffee and they're now distracted by the choreography of their elaborate potty dance? (We warned you!) Well, we're thinking it's a combination of these discomforts. But hopefully our tips and warnings have reduced your likelihood of becoming an over-anxious burnout with a great dance routine so that instead you can focus on the examples in our workbook. Speaking of which, don't you have some drills to do?

Arboreal: of or relating to trees and forests.

CHAPTER 11
Writing

NOTES:

eerrr!

OK - bear with us - this is the last section!

The writing section of the ACT is optional, as not all colleges require applicants to submit a writing score. While it is becoming increasingly required or requested, only an approximate 33% of all colleges using the ACT as their admission test currently require the writing section (this percent accounting for competitive universities); additionally, 20% of the remaining colleges *recommend* completing the essay. To check if your prospective college requires an ACT writing score, check out www.act.org/aap/writing.

Regardless of your university's preference, however, we recommend you dedicate an extra 30 minutes to the ACT and opt to write a little something-something.

While your writing score will not directly affect your reading or English score (though you will receive an additional Combined English/Writing score, which we will comment on later), an impressive essay could boost your credentials by showcasing a skill that is imperative to a successful college experience. Not to mention, you've already crawled out of bed before noon-thirty on a Saturday—might as well make the most of it.

The directions for your essay will be much longer than those listed below. As noted, the introduction will contain the presentation of a societal issue relevant to high school students.

Directions: *[Paragraph one, presentation of societal issue.]*

In your essay, take a position on this question. You may write about either one of the two points of view given, or you may present a different point of view on this question. Use specific reasons and examples to support your position.

memorize the
DIRECTIONS

Sounds pretty easy, right?

NOTES:

Slow down smarty pants. Don't be too quick to give it less credit than it deserves. Even if you're the poet laureate of your home town or the chief editor of your school newspaper, don't assume you won't need some pointers on writing an ACT essay.

Consider your 30-minute task:

1. Read the introduction
2. Contemplate and determine your stance on the subject
3. Organize your thoughts and come up with concrete, illustrative examples
4. Skipping a rough draft, carefully and thoughtfully compose an essay
5. And last, but hardly least: Proofread your work for illogical organization, rough transitions, grammatical errors, and redundancy in both thought and diction

(We're going to guess you're now prepared to humbly accept some help.) Yeah, it is a lot to do in half an hour! We have some pointers for you, though, so get those fingernails out from between your teeth.

SCORING

Essays are assessed by two ACT-certified readers who independently provide comments and score each essay on a scale of 1 to 6. If these two scores have a difference greater than one point, a third reader will step in; otherwise, the two scores are added together to produce your Writing subscore (ranging 2 to 12). The score accounts for a writer's ability to perform the following tasks in his or her essay:

- Adhere to the rules of standard written English
- Take a clear stance on the presented societal issue
- Cultivate this opinion without veering off-topic
- Utilize logical reasoning and provide supporting evidence
- Present thoughts in an organized fashion
- Make smooth transitions from one sentence or paragraph to another
- Show variety in syntax and diction

Since most test-takers will find it extremely difficult to exhibit all of these skills in under 30 minutes, earning a score of 6 from either reader is rare.

The ACT organization provides guidelines for essay readers, so scoring isn't as subjective as one might expect. Assuming you aren't interested in scoring any lower than a 4 from either of your readers, here are the benchmarks your essay must meet:

- Answer the question posed in the prompt
- Support the stance with examples and illustrations
- Show logical thought and organization
- Adequately use standard written English and avoid major errors

In addition to the previous benchmarks, a score of 5 requires your essay to:

- Provide an in-depth analysis of the topic at hand
- Utilize exceptionally concrete examples

Furthermore, to score the coveted 6, your essay must:

- Show variety in vocabulary and syntax
- Smoothly transition from one idea to another

If you're interested in seeing the acute specifics of these guidelines, or would like to see the the Combined English/Writing score table, visit www.act.org/aap/writing/sample/rubric.html.

Tips

PLAN TO PLAN

Our approach to an impressive essay is simple and straightforward: make a plan. There are two main reasons that this chapter focuses mainly on your ability to develop a solid plan: we want you to maintain realistic expectations for your essay and we want you to, well, score high.

First and foremost, the development of strong writing skills is a process that takes years of practice. If you have not previously made a special effort to become a particularly adept writer, trying to do so now would be a huge gamble. What isn't a long shot, however, is attempting to strengthen your ability to plan a good essay. This process is much less complex and can be broken down into simple, manageable steps.

Secondly, due to the tight time restrictions, 50% to 70% of students' writing falls off track as their thoughts become jumbled. The result of this derailment is disorganized and off-topic rant riddled with repetition. But what if you create a situation for yourself in which there's very little wiggle room for your writing to go haywire? Minimize the wiggle room by making and sticking to a plan that contains all of the aspects of a high-scoring essay. The plan can be viewed as a

NOTES:

skeleton that ensures your original idea remains intact, while your writing merely functions as the connective tissue. While this connective tissue is the test of a good writer, the existence of a solid frame containing a strong thesis and the supporting proof will ensure that your submission be looked upon much more kindly than a sporadic brainstorm.

Writing

PLAN FORMATION

A well-constructed plan can be developed in as little as three minutes, but we recognize that many students will need to take a full five minutes—and that's perfectly fine. A productive 20 minutes of writing from a solid outline is much better than 22 minutes worth of disconnected, irrelevant ideas. How can you be the super-productive, high-scoring essay master, you ask? Practice writing timed essays with the *BOW* method:

TAKE A BOW

OK…so we don't mean *literally* get up and begin making a scene by bowing to all your fellow test-takers: keep your butt in that seat and stop abusing our acronymns! Here's what we *really* meant…

Brainstorm. After reading the first paragraph of the prompt and knowing *exactly* what you're being asked to argue, spend 2 – 4 minutes listing any and all ideas that come to mind. This process shouldn't follow the form you were likely taught in school; don't make diagrams or free write, as these methods consume too much time. Rather, quickly list one- or two-word indicators that you can recall in the next step.

> <u>Brainstorming tip</u>: Personal observation can be one of the easiest subjects to write on, so search for correlations between your life and the matter at hand. Try to remember experiences in which you met a challenge, were faced with a moral quandary, found yourself at a major turning point, or stumbled into some sort of realization.

Furthermore, don't be afraid to elongate the catch in your fishing story or to elaborate on the epiphany you had when the bowling ball fell on your foot. Essay readers won't be performing fact checks on your stories, so feel free to be a little creative with the details and spice up your experience. As long as you aren't claiming to have caught Nessie the Loch Ness Monster or to have discovered that Newton time-traveled to steal your theory on gravity, you'll be just fine.

From this brainstorm, choose the two strongest supporting examples or illustrations and one counter-example. Your choices should steer clear of particularly emotional or offensive material (which provoke ranting) and should be logically sound (or, for the counter-example, be able to prove a logical fallacy). If you are having a difficult time choosing which examples/counterexamples to use, move on to the next step and leave "counterexample" or "example 2" blank. As you write, the correct choice may jump out at you.

NOTES:

Organize. Create your outline by assigning content to each paragraph. We suggest ordering your paragraphs thusly:

1. Introduction
    1. Inform the reader of your stance
    2. Briefly introduce example 1
    3. Present counterexample; note that it reinforces your stance
    4. Briefly introduce example 2 (strongest example)
2. Discussion of example 1
3. Discussion of counterexample(s)
4. Discussion of example 2
5. Conclusion
    1. Rephrase position
    2. Revisit examples
    3. Restate how examples apply
    4. Bang! Answer the "So what?" question

We recommend that the counterexample be sandwiched between your two positive examples. This allows you to show the logical reasoning behind your stance, deconstruct incorrect opposition, and further reinforce your stance *despite* your recognition of the other side's opinion. Additionally, by discussing your strongest example last, you have an opportunity to leave a lingering impression on your readers.

Furthermore, the "So what?" question we refer to is your chance to tell your readers what they should do or how they should feel based on what you've shown them. While it is somewhat similar to the presentation of your stance, directing your readers to take further action or adopt your viewpoint will make you sound more confident and, thus, more believable.

Write. Sticking to your outline, begin filling in your essay skeleton with the connective tissue which brings ideas to life.

As you craft your introduction, avoid simply restating the prompt. Many students begin with something of this sort:

> Directions: County locals are debating whether or not to legalize the keeping of hedgehogs as pets. Argue your position on this topic.

You: The fact that locals are debating whether or not to legalize the keeping of hedgehogs as pets is silly. My pet hedgehog is really cute!

As you can see, this is a clear case of plagiarism. (But really, why are hedgehogs not legal as pets in some states? They're too cute. After you're done studying, go check them out on the internet.) While you aren't going to be sued for infringing on intellectual property, you may end up with a painfully low score. The moral of the story: *be aware of what you're writing.*

Moreover, keep in mind that each sentence should address a single idea—that is, unless the ideas can briefly be tied together. Consider this:

> *Veni, vidi, vici.*
> - *Julius Caesar*

This quote contains three complete ideas: "I came," "I saw," and "I conquered." However, due to the masterful brevity of his words, Caesar was able to string together all three ideas without sounding like a rambling madman. But since you aren't Caesar, don't get too ambitious with your sentences. If one idea is all you can fit in one sentence, *it's all you can fit.* The last thing you want to do is to cram too much into your toga and end up exposing yourself.

NOTES:

As you construct each sentence, and toward the end of each paragraph, consider how you will transition to your next idea. It's much easier to do this mid- sentence or paragraph than when you've cemented yourself into that which you've already created.

And don't forget one of the most important steps of the writing process: proofreading! Aim to dedicate a minimum of 3 – 4 minutes to checking your work. Watch for misspellings, run-on and incomplete sentences, poorly executed transitions, and (most importantly) an unfinished conclusion paragraph.

A CRASH-COURSE IN WRITING WELL

Sure, becoming an *amazing* writer takes a lifetime of commitment—but what about simply writing well? Here are a few things to consider as you practice.

Identify Your Thesis

Before you begin your introduction, it is absolutely, positively necessary to *pinpoint a solid thesis statement. Thesis statements* are declarations of debatable stances that provide readers with expectations for the essay's development. With just that knowledge, which sentence would you say is a thesis?

Vacuums are spaces devoid of matter.

or

Home vacuums are a great way to clean your cat!

Well, our first example is more of an observation than anything. As a matter of fact, the very definition of a vacuum is a space devoid of matter. The second example, on the other hand, can *definitely* be debated. (Have you ever tried to clean your cat with a vacuum? Don't. Unless your cat is weird, in which case, you should record any and all attempts and post them on the internet.)

NOTES:

Additionally, your thesis should not be a question or a presentation. Do not ask, "Do you think I should vacuum my cat?" or proclaim, "I am going to tell you that vacuuming cats is awesome!" While you might actually be doing the latter in your paper, taking on the tone of a cat-cleaning expert is much more impressive than meekly describing your thoughts. So use your words to declare to the world how clean Fluffy is—don't just inform us of your opinion.

Lastly, choose a thesis statement that is highly specific and has further implications. This is often the most difficult task for students when they are first instructed to revise their theses as doing so entails two simultaneous processes:

1. Narrowing the scope of the paper (which, to students, sounds like "taking away stuff to write about" instead of "focusing")

and

2. applying the lesson learned from this very distinct scenario to other areas of life (or, as we call, "assessing the implications and applying them to the big picture").

NOTES:

Even though narrowing the scope of your essay will cut down on material, the substance lost isn't what you want to serve to your reader. Think about it: would you rather go to a restaurant and be served a cube of dirt that contains a raw potato (somewhere, we think), or a cleaned, baked, and dressed potato? (If you were the neighborhood kid who ate dirt as a hobby, skip to the next paragraph.) Precisely. Don't present your essay reader with a clump of earth; instead, prepare them a delicious thesis potato and dress it with the finest proofs you can afford.

As for defining a thesis's larger implications, try to determine the "moral" of your essay's discovery. If the point of your essay is to show that Ophelia is a nut-job, your reader won't have any reason to take your words to heart; if, however, you argue that Ophelia is a great example of an innocent life lost to the power-hungry maw of mankind, you're informing the reader that the blind pursuit of power places those that surround them—friends, family, lovers—in jeopardy...now *that's* something a reader would care about. Showing the importance behind your thesis helps readers consolidate all of this information into a manageable, invaluable package of wisdom which they'll hold dear.

Be Authoritative

Speaking of being an expert...Do. Not. Use. Slang. Got it? You need to sound like an authority figure, so write like you know the subject at hand. Instill confidence in the reader *(You can trust me, I know all about cat-cleaning)*. Developing a reliable voice also entails steering clear of definitive language (e.g., always, never, everyone, no one) which can corner a writer into making prolific claims beyond the scope of his or her intent *(Always surprise your cat with the vacuum; he'll never have a chance to fight back if you're already at it!)*. After all, you only have 30 minutes to back up your claim.

Formal Introductions

Your introductory paragraph should contain vague versions of the supportive details that justify your thesis. You will be writing on these topics later in greater detail, so keep it short, sweet, and vague in the introduction to avoid sounding repetitious. And if the very idea of vacuuming cats isn't fascinating enough, draw in your reader from the start with an attention grabber. Attention grabbers include quotes, *short* anecdotes, *relevant* jokes, and thought-provoking questions. But remember: a question in the introduction should not be used as your thesis statement, but as a nudge to bump your reader toward agreeing with your thesis. *(Don't you hate when your cat sheds all over your clean clothes? Boy, do I have an idea for you!)*

Using Powerful Examples

The most effective way to support your stance is to use examples that extend from general to specific. This direction of generalization takes a characteristic of a broad category and ascribes it to the category's subgroups.

> All things are yellow; this is a thing, thus this is yellow.

When moving in the opposite direction—from specific to general—faulty generalizations are often made, the most common of which is the *fallacy of composition*. One makes the fallacy of composition when a characteristic of an item within a group is assumed to be true of the group as a whole.

> This is a thing and it is yellow; thus all things must be yellow.

An attentive reader would surely recognize a logical fallacy such as this, so stick to general to specific examples.

TRANSITIONS

Well-executed transitions inform readers how to put together the information you're presenting and show how one idea is related to another and to the whole. There are quite a few transitional expressions at your disposal, so try to avoid exhausting the commonly overused ones such as *therefore* and *however*. Take a look at your arsenal:

Relationship	Transitional expression
Additional Support	also, as well, besides, equally important, further, furthermore, in addition, moreover
Cause & Effect	accordingly, consequently, hence, so, therefore, thus
Emphasis	even, indeed, in fact, of course, truly
Example	for instance, namely, specifically, to illustrate
Exception/Contrast	conversely, however, in spite of, on the contrary, nevertheless, nonetheless, notwithstanding, on the other hand, still, yet
Similarly	also, likewise, similarly

SUBJECTS AND VERBS — THE CO-DEPENDENT COUPLE

Reading through a stack of essays tends to inspire speed reading, so take care not to place too much between your subject and its verb, like we do here:

> My favorite pet *iguana*, who was given to me after my aunt told my cousin Alex that he couldn't keep it because she is terrified of amphibians, *sneezed* all over its lettuce.

Wait, who sneezed on what lettuce? Precisely. Subjects and verbs are extremely co-dependent and get lonely without each other—put too much space between them and they'll wreak havoc on your essay. Try moving that extra bit about amphibi-fear before or after the subject and verb and, for goodness sake, put them close enough to hold hands.

NOTES:

VALIANT VERBS

Often, the difference between a boring essay and an exciting tale can be identified in verb choice. Strong verbs muscle the job of both verbs *and* adjectives by *showing* action instead of merely stating an action.

Let's test this theory:

Which do you find more interesting?

The sloth moved up a tree branch and ate the colony of ants.

versus

The sloth sauntered up a tree branch and gorged upon the colony of ants.

So we're comparing two different sets of verbs: *moved* and *sauntered*, and *ate* and *gorged*. *Moving* simply implies a change in location whereas *sauntering* entails movement at a slow, leisurely pace. *Eating* has the same drab of a description-less action, but *gorging* implies a greedy, over-zealous consumption. (So, what do you think? *Moved* and *ate*, or *sauntered* and *gorged*?)

Being conscious of your verb choice can do wonders for your essay. And we mean this in more than one way...

ACTIVE VERBS

Poorly chosen verbs also can put readers to sleep by making sentences passive, inactive couch potatoes. An active sentence has its subject performing the verb, but a passive sentence has the subject sitting stagnant while an extraneous (and often unnamed) force performs the verb onto the subject. The difference is illustrated below.

> The pedestrians were being run over by the enraged bus driver!

Versus

> The enraged bus driver ran over the pedestrians!

In the first example, the *direct object* of the sentence ("the pedestrians," the ones *receiving* the action) are acted upon ("being run over"). In the second example, the *subject* of the sentence ("the enraged bus driver," the one *performing* the action) is described as having performed the action (ran over). Therefore, the second sentence is considered active while the first is considered inactive.

Here's another example of an inactive sentence:

This dainty, red tricycle will be ridden by a bear!

To determine if the sentence is active or passive, ask yourself:

- Who or what is the main subject?
- What main action is performed?
- What is the direct object?

Active sentences follow the order of subject-verb-object. Passive sentences, however, are reversed and generally use a linking verb (i.e. is, am, are, was, were, be, being, been) as the main verb.

So how about that example – is it active or passive? Our subject is a bear, the action is ridden, and the object is tricycle. Unfortunately for our sentence, though, these items come in the reverse order, thus making our sentence passive. So how can we fix this? Reverse them, of course!

A bear is going to ride this dainty, red tricycle!

Notice how active sentences also coincide with brief sentences? (It's not a co-inki-dink.)

HEINOUS HOMONYMS

Sometimes the meanings of our words get lost when we try to transcribe them. One way this happens is by the confusion of homonyms: words that look and/or sound similar but have different meanings. Most of the time these blunders are just silly (and not silly in the sense that your readers will chuckle lovingly and praise your effort with 6's). Sometimes, however, these homonyms can turn an honest mistake into a heinous abuse of the English language. To keep you angelic in the eyes of your readers, we put together a list of the most common misused words and phrases (though some have been omitted as we've already discussed them under the English section).

Accept & Except:

Accept is a verb that means "to receive" and *except* is a preposition which means "to exclude."

> I will gladly *accept* any and all high-fives that come my way.

> After all, high-fives are awesome (well, *except* when they're doled out by people who don't wash their hands after flushing—gross!)

Allusion & Illusion:

Both of these homonyms are nouns, but an *allusion* is an implied reference or subtle hint at something and an *illusion* is a trick of perception (generally visual).

After making numerous *allusions* to the greatness of authentic Asian food, I expected my date to bring me to one of the local sushi parlors.

When I opened my eyes, however, I could only pray that Burger Master was just an *illusion* and that at *any* second, the drive-thru would dissipate and our true destination would appear.

illusion

Anyway & Any Way:

Anyway is an adverb which means "in any case," or "regardless." (Side note: can an adverb be plural? *No!* It is never, ever, *ever* to be written as *anyways*.) *Any way* is an adjective-noun duo meaning "whatever means/direction."

> This coffee is cold and bitter, but we are going to drink it *anyway*.

> If there's *any way* for us to drive to NYC in one night, it must entail coffee—and lots of it.

Climactic & Climatic:

Climactic refers to the peak of intensity whereas *climatic* refers to environmental conditions.

> The most *climactic*, nail-biting scene in the movie occurred when the polar bear fell into the icy water.

> The changing *climatic* conditions were, as the film explained, due to the depletion of the Earth's ozone.

NOTES:

Elicit & Illicit:

Elicit is a verb meaning "to draw out or evoke" and *illicit* is an adjective which means "disallowed," be it for moral or legal reasons.

> Do whatever you can to *elicit* a confession from the Trench Coat Flasher suspect.

> We simply cannot allow him to run around performing such an *illicit* act in public!

Emigrate & Immigrate:

Both of these words refer to the exchange of people from one area to another; however, *emigrate* means "to leave a country" and *immigrate* means "to enter a foreign country." Much like *affect* and *effect* (remember these guys from the English chapter?), emigrate and immigrate can remembered in a chronological-alphabetical order.

> With no opportunity in sight, the family woefully packed their bags to *emigrate* from their home land.

> As they *immigrated* into their new country, the children were dumbfounded by the towering height of skyscrapers.

For all intents and purposes:

Yes, *intents* and purposes. Please don't ever write "For all intensive purposes;" the colloquialism is, and always has been, "For all *intents and purposes.*" That is all.

Principal and Principle:

Both nouns, *principal* refers to the leader of a school or other organization and *principle* refers to fundamental law or truth (i.e. your morals). To keep these two straight, ask yourself: who can you be *pals* with? The only one capable of being a pal: your princi*pal*.

> Students weren't exactly fans of the school *principal*, Ms. Oxford.

> As far as they were concerned, Ms. Oxford was too concerned with her *principles* of education and not concerned enough with the value of recess.

Supposed to & Used to:

Both of these *end in a "D."* They are alternatives for "meant/intended to" and "formerly," respectively. Even if you're forecasting into the future *(I'm supposed to toilet paper my coach's house tonight.)*, note that you're still saying that you're *meant to* do something. (Look, English was this way before we wrote this—don't blame us.)

Toward:

If you're prone to saying *towards*, with an *s*, don't beat up on yourself. It's an old-school, British thing to do. While they're both correct, the democratic Grammar General of the United States says, "March on toward a better future—off with the *s*!"

Than & Then:

Than is a conjunction that is used to express an inequality between two or more items. *Then* most frequently is used as an adverb to mean "at that time."

There are many more mullets in this room *than* there are mustaches.

If this is acceptable, and if I shouldn't be seriously concerned, *then* I must have accidentally time traveled to 1982.

To, Too, & Two:

You knew it was coming, didn't you? If you haven't yet sorted these three, snap to it! Right...*now.*

To is used as a preposition, in which it precedes a noun, and as an infinitive, in which it precedes a verb. *Too* should only be used when it can be swapped with *also* or *excessively.* Period. *Two* is a number. It means one more than one, i.e., 2.

> You really need *to* study and get this to/too/two thing figured out.

> There are far *too* many people who can't keep them straight.

> I'll give you *two* more seconds to think about it before we move on.

> (O.K., move on.)

Your & You're:

Your is the possessive form of you. *You're* is a contraction for *you are.*

> Have I told you lately that *your* hair looks great?

> Oh, and *you're* still going to give me those concert tickets, right?

> (Totally not related. I swear.)

Who, Which, & That:

These guys are tricky because they're all pronouns with similar usage; so, pay close attention.

When writing formally (i.e., for the ACT), *who* should be used whenever referring to a person. When referring to a thing or concept, *which* is generally preferred. However, *that* is used when following the pronouns *all, few, little, many, much, none,* and any pronoun ending in *thing* (e.g., everything, anything, etc.)

> And *who* do you think stole the cookies from the cookie jar?

> Well, the thief devoured the *batch, which* we'd sneakily laced with laxatives.

> After last week's sugar cookie heist, we thought it best to prepare a *few* treats *that* will surely give away our burglar!

Who's & Whose: *Who's* is a contraction for *who* is and *whose* is the possessive form of *who*. If you can remember *your* and *you're*, you can remember these guys.

Who's prepared to go camping?

Also, *whose* tent are we using?

So what did we learn? You don't want to be the perpetrator of a heinous homonym crime: the ACT readers won't appreciate this abomination against the English language.

WRAPPING IT UP

Students frequently reach the conclusion of their essay with an exhausted mind and give up the good fight. This is *so* not the answer. The conclusion is your last chance to plead your case and will be the most memorable piece of your essay, simply for the fact that it will be the last thing your reader "hears" from you.

NOTES:

As you construct your conclusion, rephrase your thesis statement (do *not* simply restate it; this will send you packing to the Dept. of Redundancy Department).
It is also helpful to refresh the reader's memory by recapping your argument and briefly revisiting your supportive details.

For an extra bang, try to make a prediction of future actions or thoughts on your topic, present a possible solution to the issue at hand, offer a recommendation for further involvement, or end with another anecdote.

Dept. of Redundancy Department

NOTES:

Tips

ADDITIONAL WRITING TIPS

- Don't be tempted to get too creative and write something *inspired* by the prompt. Respond by directly addressing the issue at hand.

- Take an unwavering, clear stance on the topic. Absolutely do *not* stand on the fence—be on one side or the other. While you should address a counterexample, avoid sounding too sympathetic (you are, after all, claiming that it is wrong).

- Visual aesthetics are important when it comes to your handwriting. Print, don't use cursive, and keep control over the legibility of your essay. If your handwriting degrades into chicken-scratch, your essay readers might end up struggling just to decipher your essay and henceforth not take too kindly to your ideas.

- When correcting your work, it is entirely acceptable to ~~cross out~~ words or sentences and rewrite the material nearby with a clear indication of the amendment's location. This method saves you from cramming (and thus making your words illegible) and from wasting your time on erasing.

Keep it
neat.

Tips

The body of each paragraph should end with a clear connection to your stance; do not count on your readers to figure it out—just come out and say how your examples are relevant.

Utilizing college-level vocabulary is a great way to impress your essay reader—and so is utilizing a mixture of complex, compound, and simple sentences.

As stated before, personal observations can be great examples. However, try to minimize the over-use of "me" and "I", and avoid using recent occurrences in your life. It is better to write about something that happened in a distant-enough past so that you can present a much more rational, objective point of view. Older experiences also open up the possibility for discussing your feelings at the time of the event *and* your more mature feelings in hindsight.

Tips

- As always, make concrete correlations between your observation and the topic at hand. If these correlations can be best shown by a modified version of the truth, tell a little lie (but keep it realistic!). Your essay only has a short time to impact your readers—do what it takes to grab their attention.

- Avoid, at all cost to your integrity as an advanced writer, *not* coming out and stating the obvious no matter how obvious it already seems to you. The art of subtlety is *not* your friend on the ACT essay.

- Don't be satisfied with a short essay. As concise a writer as you may be, your essay's length will have an impact on your score. An ideal essay is comprised of about five paragraphs, approximately five sentences each, and contains anywhere from 350 to 450 words. But before you start freaking out: the ACT Organization makes it clear that zero points are awarded for following a specific format or reaching a specific length; what *is* important, they stress, is that your writing be clear, cohesive, and direct.

- Steer clear of digression: use your outline to stay on topic and to track how much more writing you will need to do.

Tips

✐ Prior to the big day, you should have completed a minimum of two practice essays. Based on these practice runs, you should have two full essays with concrete examples and spectacular verbiage before you even set foot in the exam room. If possible, try to incorporate pieces of these writings into your exam essay.

✐ If you're having a hard time getting yourself to practice writing, consider this: college admission officers have every right to request a copy of your essay. If you do poorly on the ACT writing section, it might negate the awesome letter you wrote on your college application, so don't slack off on the essay just because you're a generally competent writer or because you're "burnt out" from the past three hours of ACT torture.

Strategies

One spiffy way to beef-up your writing skills is to keep a journal. If it doesn't drive you absolutely insane, write in pencil instead of on a computer or in pen. This way, you can become well-acquainted with the same mind-to-paper processes you'll be using on the big day. Your journal should contain your own internal thoughts, your accounts of and responses to current events, and your assessments of big ideas and beliefs. You probably won't want to write in proper form on a daily basis, but make an effort to complete a weekly or bi-weekly basis that you would be proud to present. This means crafting a strong thesis statement, making sound arguments, refuting counterclaims, and communicating in standard written English.

✐ (Even though we know you wouldn't *dare* allow yourself to ramble in the essay...) Remember how in the English section we told you that fluff is the worst? Well, it's actually the bane of an essay reader's existence. With piles of hand written essays to read, the ACT essay readers quickly become spiteful toward wordiness and filler material. Instead of doing everything in your power to make your essay readers hate you, create beefy paragraphs by illustrating your argument through the use of concrete examples and by explicitly stating the sometimes obvious connections.

Ask any notable author and he or she will tell you that the best way to become a better writer is through *practice*; so, get to writing! In addition to drafting your first copy, always revisit your "completed" work to practice the editing process. By revising your own work, you'll gain a sense of your weaknesses and know exactly how to accommodate for these when composing future essays. And for goodness sake, allow yourself to be creative.

Have some fun!

CHAPTER 12

Recap!

NOTES:

First of all: you made it! Unless you're cheating and just trying to get all of the tips out of the text *without actually reading it* (shame on you), you've just finished reading a comprehensive overview of the ACT! Congratulations, you're now one ginormous step closer to success!

(Go ahead, do a dance. We'll wait.)

(Nice.)

So, we've told you about the five easily conquerable factors that stand between you and your full potential:

1) little-to-no exposure to the test format and content

2) a lack of test-taking strategies

3) an abundance of stress and anxiety

4) poor time-management skills

5) sleep deprivation

NOTES:

But, hopefully, we've also shared with you some helpful hints on overcoming these barriers.

First and foremost, we threw out some of the pesky ACT myths that trap otherwise well-prepared students:

Contrary to rumor and urban legend:

- There aren't any trick questions, but there are answers that are *sneakily* close to the correct answer.

- Each question has only *one* correct answer.

- Correct answers do not follow any pattern, so don't waste your time seeking a hidden image on the bubble sheet.

- All choices are equally likely to occur. Contrary to an oddly popular belief, C is not always your best bet. (Okay, seriously, where did this urban legend come from?)

- The directions will be the same from one test to another. Memorizing these directions can save you a precious minute or two per section.

- Questions are generally arranged in random difficulty. This is a time trap, so don't allow a difficult one to throw you off from the get-go.

NOTES:

Additionally, we provided these tips to help you manage your time efficiently:

- Know the directions before the test day. Wait, didn't we say that already? *But you still haven't memorized them?* Ahem.

- Bring a watch.

- Have each section's end-time written on the cover of your test booklet.

- Complete an entire page of questions in your booklet prior to transferring them to your bubble sheet.

- Unless a hand cramp requires your fingers to do some yoga, don't put down your pencil.

- Easy questions have the same point-value as difficult questions; when appropriate, guess on those hard questions and move on.

- Yep, guessing is A-OK. There are no point deductions for bad answers, only point gains for right answers.

- ~~Strike out~~ obviously bad answers and don't bother revisiting them.

- <u>Underline</u> important information such as logic reversal words, cause-and-effect relationships, and key terms.

- Take super-duper brief notes in the margins of all reading passages to quickly relocate information while answering questions.

- Seemingly difficult questions can be simplified by restating them in your own words.

Furthermore, we gave some tips to help with each specific section of the test. If you haven't done so yet, revisit each section's tips and read the lists in their full detail. This recap section is meant only as a *reminder* of things you already know.

NOTES:

ENGLISH TIPS

- Prior to reading prose carefully, *quickly* scan the entire piece to make a forecast of what you'll be reading. Anticipating what is to come will make you more receptive to forthcoming information.

- Anticipating will also give you expectations for the passage, making oddball sentences stick out like sore thumbs.

- Know what is important while you read by glancing at questions *before* performing your thorough reading.

- Be sensitive to the tones of passages so that you'll be able to notice inconsistencies.

- Listen to your instincts when they tell you that *something* about what you've just read is odd. Beware of choosing "No change" if you feel that something is amiss, be it for logical sequence, wording, or otherwise.

NOTES:

- Good writing is concise writing. Alter sentences to remove irrelevant information, needless repetition, and wordiness. *When in doubt, take it out.*

- If a portion of a passage is <u>underlined</u>, meticulously re-read it. You will likely be answering a question or two regarding this information.

GOT
THAT?

MATH TIPS

- Write, calculate, and scribble all over your test booklet. This section gives you plenty of white space; use it to draw diagrams and perform calculations. (Remember: Calculations performed on paper are less likely to contain silly errors than those performed mentally.)

- Get artsy and draw diagrams to help visualize the problem at hand, *especially* when working on a distance or dimension problem.

- When the diagrams aren't drawn to scale, if you don't know the answer, take the time to redraw them to scale. This may help you "eyeball" your way to the correct answer.

- Backsolving, i.e. plugging in answers and checking the outcome, is amazingly efficient for complex algebraic computations.

- Intimidating geometry problems can almost almost *always* be simplified by breaking them down into smaller, easier steps.

- Carefully read word problems and <u>underline</u> exactly what you are being asked. The last thing you want to do is get the math right, but get the question wrong because you weren't paying attention to what they were asking.

- **DRT** = **D**istance = **R**ate × **T**ime

- **TAN** = **T**otal = **A**verage × **N**umber

- SOH CAH TOA:

$$sin = \frac{opposite}{hypotenuse} \qquad cos = \frac{adjacent}{hypotenuse} \qquad tangent = \frac{opposite}{adjacent}$$

- Some helpful values: $\pi \approx 3.14 \quad \sqrt{2} \approx 1.4 \quad \sqrt{3} \approx 1.7$

- Know how to use your calculator and bring an extra set of batteries. (Better safe than sorry.)

READING TIPS

- Don't try to get a doctorate in each passage. Just get a handle on the big picture.

- Pay extra attention to the first and last paragraph as well as the first and last sentence of each paragraph.

- <u>Underline</u> important information such as the main idea, logic reversal vocabulary, names and places, words relating to sequence, and words relating to relationships.

- Know your reading speed prior to test-day so that you can make realistic estimations of the amount of time you can dedicate to each passage.

- Adjust your speed as you read: slow down for the author's objective and perspective and speed up for supporting details.

- Dedicate more time to the questions and answers than to the passage itself.

- Only choose answers that are stated *explicitly* in the prose.

- Be keen to absolute language (it's usually a trick!).

- Formulate your responses to questions prior to looking through your options.

- Only general questions (i.e., ones regarding tone, theme, or overall message) should be answered without revisiting the passage.

- As for those general questions, if the answer is not immediately clear, circle them and move on; answering other questions may give you a clearer idea of the passage.

- Logical inference questions will be denoted with the words *imply, infer, inference,* or *suggest.*

- If you've completed enough workouts to know that reading all four passages is a difficult task for you due to time constraints, carefully read three passages and make educated guesses on the fourth. This is truly a great strategy!

- When faced with a time crunch, seek questions that come with a line-reference.

NOTES:

SCIENCE TIPS

- Don't try to understand fully the science presented on the ACT. Rather, aim to gain a general understanding of the passage. Ask yourself:
    1. What is the purpose of the experiment?
    2. What is being tested and why?
    3. What are the variables and constants?
    4. How is the outcome affected by each variable change?

- <u>Underline</u> *italicized* words to make them stand out more.

- Circle units of measurement (*mph, inches*), key words (*decrease, increase*), and reversal words (*except, not*).

- Establish a form of shorthand which you'll use to take notes in the margins.

- Do *not* skip general understanding questions in this section. If you cannot answer these, you'll have one heck of a time answering more detailed questions.

NOTES:

- Choose an option that actually answers the question being asked, and not one that merely states something true about the passage.

- When you come across complex jargon, ignore the intricacy of the language and consider the big picture.

- For questions that refer to an image, skim the questions prior to doing any reading; the accompanying reading may be superfluous.

- ~~Cross out~~ answers that contradict the passage or draw on the tendency to extrapolate data.

- Don't select an answer that isn't explicitly supported in the passage.

- Experiments reported on the ACT are *never* flawed. If asked if a researcher made a mistake or if the experiment itself was flawed, ignore the YES options.

- Save the science reading passages for last. Those that have to do with charts and graphs will be much easier and faster to answer correctly.

- At the five-minute mark, seek out data representation questions, which can be answered much more swiftly than passage questions.

NOTES:

Essay

WRITING TIPS

- Respond directly to the prompt; do not write something vaguely inspired by it.

- Take a stance and maintain your opinion throughout your essay.

- Print your essay neatly. Cursive and chicken scratch are difficult to read!

- Feel free to ~~cross out~~ words or sentences in your essay and use an arrow to insert the rewritten pieces. Erasing and/or cramming in material can be messy and time consuming.

- Draw clear connections between each paragraph and your thesis.

- Use a mixture of complex, compound, and simple sentences.

- Try to utilize college-level vocabulary.

- Employ personal observation in your essay, but avoid overusing "me" and "I." The best personal observations are those from your past.

- Modified versions of your experience can boost the impact of your story. Just be careful not to over-exaggerate and give away your fib.

- State the obvious. Subtlety is *not* your friend on the ACT.

- Aim for an essay length of 350 to 450 words; this length is generally comparable to five paragraphs, each containing four to five sentences.

- Use your outline as an anchor to keep you from drifting off-topic.

- Complete two practice essays prior to test day. Try to integrate pieces of them into your ACT essay submission.

- Practice writing on a regular basis by keeping a journal.

- Absolutely do *not* add fluff to your essay just to make it look longer!

Lastly, but of the highest order of importance,

Practice! Practice! Practice!

"But I've practiced so much that I've exhausted your workbook," you say? Awesome! Jump on your computer and go to www.act.org for more practice tests. Even if you only increase your composite score by one *measly* point, you'll be ranked higher than 100,000 other students nationwide. That's right: 1 point and you're more desirable to colleges than 100,000 students (psst, remember how we said that colleges express their desire in acceptance letters and *free money?* They do!). Interested?

Think about it…if you decide that the opportunity for a lifetime of success <u>is</u>, in fact, worth a mere 20 hours of your youth, then you need to make the commitment! And we're not just talking about having reached this last page; *we're saying you need to study* so that, come the big day, you'll be able to remember all the amazing stuff we gave you here.

So, this is not good-bye. Keep this book handy as it can serve as a great future reference. In college, you will be expected to do some self-educating; this means reading things that may not be specifically on your curriculum lists, and writing outside of your assignments—just like we had you do here.

In a strange way, this "outside class" reading and researching is liberating. It means you are finally escaping the intellectual confines of high school. In closing, we wish you all the best as you move toward your new collegiate adventure. We would bid you adieu with a "good luck" wish, but if you have followed our advice, we know you won't need it.

Go get 'em!

BLANK CHARTS

STUDY SCHEDULE

Week	Sun	Mon	Tue	Wed	Thu	Fri	Sat

Key: **E**nglish – **M**ath – **R**eading – **S**cience – **W**riting

PRACTICE TEST SCORES

Assessment Date	Composite	English	Math	Reading	Science	Writing